Linguistic Inquiry
Monograph Fourteen

On the Definition of Word

Anna Maria Di Sciullo and
Edwin Williams

On the Definition of Word

Linguistic Inquiry Monographs
Samuel Jay Keyser, general editor

On the Definition of Word   Anna-Maria Di Sciullo
and Edwin Williams

The MIT Press
Cambridge, Massachusetts
London, England

This book was set in Times New Roman by Asco Trade Typesetting Ltd., Hong Kong, and printed and bound by Halliday Lithograph in the United States of America.

Library of Congress Cataloging-in-Publication Data

Di Sciullo, Anna-Maria, 1951–
  On the definition of word.

  (Linguistic inquiry monographs; 14)
  Bibliography: p.
  Includes index.
  1. Word (Linguistics)   I. Williams, Edwin.   II. Title.   III. Series.
P128.W67D5   1987   415   86-27206
ISBN 0-262-04091-3
ISBN 0-262-54047-9 (pbk.)

Contents

P
128
.W67
D5
1987

Series Foreword

We are pleased to present this monograph as the fourteenth in the series *Linguistic Inquiry Monographs*. These monographs will present new and original research beyond the scope of the article, and we hope they will benefit our field by bringing to it perspectives that will stimulate further research and insight.

Originally published in limited edition, the *Linguistic Inquiry Monograph* series is now available on a much wider scale. This change is due to the great interest engendered by the series and the needs of a growing readership. The editors wish to thank the readers for their support and welcome suggestions about future directions the series might take.

Samuel Jay Keyser
for the Editorial Board

On the Definition of Word

The Notion "Word"

There are three different ideas of what a word is. Our purpose here is to sort them out, and in this introductory section we will do this in a preliminary way. The notion central to this text concerns the *form* of a certain set of objects; the definition of this set is the theory of morphological form. The theory defines the set by means of a set of atoms (morphemes) and rules of combination (affixing, compounding). We will call the members of this set *morphological objects* and assert that the central task of morphology is to determine the laws of form that determine membership in this set. Just as morphology has atoms, so does syntax, and words are commonly taken to be the atoms of syntax. We will call words in this sense *syntactic atoms*. This notion of word is conceptually and factually distinct from that of word as "morphological object." We will discuss an important class of items that are syntactic atoms (insertable in X^0 slots in syntactic structures) but that do not have morphological form (in fact they have syntactic form). Finally, the third notion of word we want to discuss is the one from which most confusion about words derives—the notion of words as the "listed" units of language. For this notion of word, which we believe to be of no interest to the grammarian (though perhaps it is to the psychologist), we coin the term *listeme*. We will show that the listemes of a language correspond to neither the morphological objects nor the syntactic atoms of a language.

Morphology and syntax are similar in that each has a set of atoms and some rules of combination. It is our thesis that the difference between these two subtheories is exactly a difference in the atoms and in the properties of the rules of formation. There are of course other imaginable ideas of what constitutes the difference between syntax and morphology. For example, one might conceive of morphology as a theory of the lexicon, an innocuous-sounding conception but one from which we feel flows a great deal of confusion. Another perhaps related idea of the difference is that syntax is a characterization of the "productive" aspects of language and morphology a characterization of the semi- or unproductive aspects. These views tend to equate *listeme* and *morphological object*. Under such a view, the following diagram characterizes the "ideal" language:

	Word	Phrase
Listed	yes	no
Unlisted	no	yes

Of course there are exceptions in every cell of this diagram. The question is, Are these exceptions deviations from an ideal, or is the ideal misconceived in the first place? A difficult question.

For example, there are vast veins of productive (and so we assume unlisted) morphology, such as the words ending in -*ness* in English. In addition, there are unproductive and therefore listed veins of idiomatic syntactic constructions, such as the verb-particle construction in English. In fact we can show that all cells in this diagram are substantially filled and should be marked "yes."

But our objection to the diagram is more fundamental than these factual observations would suggest. The diagram itself, however the cells are filled, is an artifact of the confusion we seek to address.

The distinction between word and phrase is a distinction in the theory of grammar. The listed/unlisted distinction has nothing to do with grammar. Syntax and morphology are both recursive definitions of sets of objects—but of different sets, with different atoms and different rules of combination. These are the only differences the grammarian need acknowledge.

The most immediate consequence of this view is that productivity and listedness are not grammatical concepts. We will explore this in chapter 1, where we will examine the property of "listedness." A second consequence is that the lexicalist hypothesis (which we call here the *thesis of the atomicity of words*) is not a principle of grammar but rather a consequence of the conception that grammar contains two subparts, with different atoms and different rules of formation. We will take this up in chapters 3 and 4, which concern the notion "syntactic atom." In chapter 2 we will present a substantive account of the laws and rules of word formation, which we take to constitute the notion "morphological object."

In sum, then, we postulate three empirically and conceptually distinct notions of word: listeme, syntactic atom, and morphological object. In fact, though, there is a fourth, which we will essentially ignore here: the notion of phonological word. We take it up briefly at the end of chapter 4 mainly to draw the contrast with the other senses of word.

Chapter 1
Listeme: The Property of Listedness

Knowledge of language involves in some way a knowledge of particular linguistic objects—for example, the word *transmission* and the knowledge that it (1) has a certain morphological form and (2) refers to a part of a car; that *take to task* has a certain syntactic form and means "rebuke". To the extent that an object does not have the form or interpretation specified by the recursive definitions of the objects of the language, that object and its properties must be "memorized." We have dubbed such memorized objects *listemes*, and this property of being memorized, *listedness*. Our overall point is that listedness is no more intrinsically characteristic of words than it is of phrases. Some words and some phrases are listed, but infinitely many of each are not.

If conceived of as the set of listemes, the lexicon, is incredibly boring by its very nature. It contains objects of no single specifiable type (words, VPs, morphemes, perhaps intonation patterns, and so on), and those objects that it does contain are there because they fail to conform to interesting laws. The lexicon is like a prison—it contains only the lawless, and the only thing that its inmates have in common is lawlessness.

This view of the lexicon is quite unfriendly to most current proposals, which by and large can be traced to the influential view of Jackendoff (1975). According to Jackendoff, all words of a language are listed in the lexicon, whether or not they conform completely to the laws of form and meaning for words. The rules of morphology are conceived of as redundancy rules, by means of which the "cost" of a lexical item is computed. Those that are totally predictable will have no cost.

We do not take issue with the view that the "cost" of a word is a function of its deviation from the rules of morphology. As noted, a structured item is easier to memorize than an unstructured one. But we do take issue with the idea that the rules of morphology are essentially redundancy rules over ı finite set of objects in a way that syntactic rules are not. To us this makes no more sense than to say that VP → V NP is a redundancy rule over the set of VPs, most but of course not all of which have zero redundancy.

Jackendoff acknowledges that there are phrases in the lexicon (idioms) and that "possible words" that are not in the lexicon can be created and used, but these aberrations do not deter him from conceiving of the lexicon as a list of all the words of a language, and of the rules of morphology as a "theory" of that list.

A related view that we reject is the idea that "productivity" is characteristic of syntax and "unproductivity" is characteristic of morphology. Fabb (1984, 38), for example, explicitly considers this a criterial difference, and many others implicitly consider it as such. Selkirk (1981), for example, proposes that productive compounds are derived in syntax and unproductive or idiosyncratic ones are listed in the lexicon. In our view, to the extent that productivity is phenomenally perceived to distinguish syntax and morphology, this is something to explain, not something that follows from the intrinsic nature of these two systems, and the explanation is not all that interesting (see section 1.2.3).

Another related view that we reject is the idea that the lexicon has structure. As mentioned, it is simply a collection of the lawless, and there neither can nor should be a theory directly about it, for it can only be understood in terms of the laws it fails to obey. This is not to say that the space of words in a language is not structured—in fact the space of words has a rich structure, imposed first by the rules of word formation and second by the paradigmatic matrices that words enter into (see Williams 1981). But the lexicon contains only some of the words that enter into this structure (the ones that do it least well), and it contains much else besides. In sum we reject the idea that listedness is a grammatical property—the lexicon is a collection of semigrammatical objects, some of them words and others phrases. The set of listed items has no structure, and the property of being a member of this set is no more essential to the nature of words than it is to the nature of phrases.

Of course this is not to say that knowledge of the listed items of a language is not part of knowledge of that language. Rather, if we think of the rules of formation for words and phrases as defining the grammatical items of the language, then we might regard the lexicon as containing a finite list of some semigrammatical objects that are a part of the language.

In the next two sections we will explore somewhat the reasons for distinguishing the lexicon from the space of words of a language. We will concentrate on the two important types of case for which these two concepts fail to coincide: (1) the listed syntactic objects and (2) the unlisted (and unlistable) morphological objects.

1.1 Listed Syntactic Objects

The listed syntactic objects are the idioms. Although these are like some words in that their meanings cannot be compositionally computed, this very feature makes them unlike most words.

As far as we can see, there is nothing more to say about them than that (1) they are syntactic objects and (2) they are listed because of their failure to have a predictable property (usually their meaning).

It is not trivial to say that an item is a syntactic object: it means that the item is a syntactic unit of some kind—an NP, VP, and so on. It is certainly conceivable that some concatenation of words that was not a unit could be an idiom, or that some particular string of words, such as *park saw* in *The man in the park saw the woman*, could contribute an unpredictable element of meaning to a sentence, but idioms do not work like this—they are always units.

They do not always look like units. For example, the VP *take NP to task* looks like a discontinuous unit, wrapped around the object NP—in fact it has been proposed (by Emonds (1969) for one) that *take to task* is a complex V and not a VP at all (with *to task* extraposed by a rule).

This description, which would enormously complicate the morphological notion "verb," is not forced on us, because we can assign the idiom the following structure:

(1)

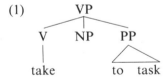

This idiom contains an unfilled position, the NP object; nevertheless, it is formally a VP and functions as one when inserted for the node VP in a sentence.

There are many such VPs in English (*take in hand, push too far*), all of whose properties follow if they are viewed simply as listed VPs. There are probably as many such VPs as there are noncompositional words ending in *-ion*, so this should not be viewed as a minor appendix to the dictionary.

Another set of such VPs in English consists of verb-particle constructions (*look up, throw up*, and so on), which are listed VPs consisting of a V, a particle, and an (optional) open NP position. We will discuss this system shortly.

The discontinuity these VPs exhibit follows from allowing one free open position. This need not be in the object position—it can be inside the direct object position (for example, *bite NP's head off*). In general it can probably be anywhere.

French exhibits a more interesting discontinuity—idioms that include clitics such as *en* (see Di Sciullo 1983):

(2) [en mettre plein la vue]$_{VP}$
    'to impress greatly'
    [en voir de toutes les couleurs]$_{VP}$
    'to have a hard time'

These clitics can wind up in S-Structure separated from the rest of the idiom, as in the following examples:

(3) Jean en voit de toutes les couleurs
    Jean en a vu de toutes les couleurs
    Jean en fait voir de toutes les couleurs

The separation is exactly what one would expect if the VPs in (2) were inserted for VP nodes in S and cliticization were then to apply. Incidentally, these apparently provide strong evidence for a cliticization rule—the clitic attaches to the first finite verb, whether or not it is part of the idiom. Again, the discontinuity is no obstacle to calling these syntactic units, specifically, VPs.

Calling idioms listed syntactic units means not only that they will be units in the first place but also that they will have the internal structure of other syntactic units in the language and will behave as other units do in syntax; and, as is clear from these examples, this is the case.

We are further led by this view to expect to find listed syntactic units of all kinds—NP, AP, PP, VP, S—and we do:

(4) AP   all wet
    PP   in the dark about NP
    S   the cat has got NP's tongue
    N'   that son of a bitch
    NP   The Big Apple

The great wealth of such expressions in languages substantiates half of the view that there is nothing special about listed words. In fact there are listemes among all the syntactic categories, perhaps as many as there are words. Further, these listemes have quite regular internal syntax, syntax of the kind given by phrasal syntax, not by morphology.

1.2 Unlisted Morphological Objects

The second part of our argument that there is no correspondence between listedness and morphological objecthood is the demonstration that there are unlisted morphological objects. Actually this is quite widely recognized; all theories of morphology acknowledge, for example, the ability of speakers to make up new words. Thus Halle (1973) cites the series of words *anti-missile missile, anti-anti-missile missile missile,* and so on—an infinite series of words, each with a determinate meaning different from that of all the others.

Most views, though, attach grammatical significance to the use of a new word—when a speaker makes up a new word, he changes his grammar by adding the word to his lexicon, even if the word's form and meaning are completely determined by regular rule (see, for example, Jackendoff 1975). But in our view the listedness of a regular form is of no grammatical significance, and whether or not it is listed will vary from speaker to speaker, determined by such factors as its frequency of use in the speaker's daily life.

Most views of morphology distinguish it from syntax in some way that has to do with productivity: use of a new (but regular) syntactic phrase does not result in that phrase being listed in the dictionary, but the use of a new word will. This, so the story goes, is because syntax is inherently productive, whereas morphology is inherently nonproductive or only marginally or spottily productive. This difference is related to a second difference: "blocking" of one form by another (in the sense of Aronoff 1976) only obtains among morphological objects, not among syntactic objects.

In the next two sections we will argue that neither of these distinctions between syntax and morphology is real—that both systems are productive in the same way and that blocking, to the extent that it holds at all, holds in both systems and in fact holds across both systems.

1.2.1 Productivity

It is often noted (and great consequence is attached to it) that *-ness* is more productive than *-ion*. Thus practically any adjective can have *-ness* attached, but only a few select verbs have nominalizations in *-ion* (*breakion, *cution, *bition, *killion). These two affixes are said to differ in productivity. We might imagine assigning a productivity index to each affix, where we arrive at the index by dividing the number of forms that the affix actually attaches to by the total number of items belonging to the part of speech (C) that the item attaches to:

(5) $P_{af} = \dfrac{\text{size (X-af)}}{\text{size (C)}}$

But as Aronoff (1976) understood, the productivity of an affix is not uniform across an entire part of speech; -ion, for example, is highly productive (in fact P = 1) for verbs of the form X-*ate* (*emancipate, calibrate*). This provokes us to ask, Why compute productivity over a part of speech? Why not a smaller domain (verbs ending in -*ate*) or a larger domain (the entire lexicon)? Is there any answer to this that is not arbitrary?

Suppose that we compute productivity within the contextual restrictions of the affix itself. Thus -*ness* is restricted to As, so the productivity is computed with respect to size (A). But -*ion* is restricted to the Latinate subvocabulary in English. In that subvocabulary -*ion* is extremely productive; perhaps P = 1.

It may be objected that this computation of P_{-ion} is artificial because the only way to identify the Latinate subvocabulary is to see what -*ion* attaches to in the first place. But in this case the charge is not true; there are other ways to identify the subvocabulary. For example, consider the class of words that -*ive* attaches to. The affix -*ion* is 100 percent productive across that independently identified class. Actually the Latinate vocabulary is a closed class to start with, but -*ion* is extremely productive within that class, just as -*ness* is productive across its class (the class of all As). The only difference between -*ion* and -*ness* is that -*ness* is initially defined for a larger class.

In fact -*ion* is productive in the most basic sense of the word—it can be used to make up new words. Of course the base word must be of the right type, which happens to be a relatively closed class to begin with, so most of the possible -*ion* attachments already "exist." But if one encounters a new verb ending in -*ate* (say, *lucubrate*), one does not have to guess, one knows, that a word can be derived from it by adding -*ion* (*lucubration*).

It may seem that we want to regard -*ion* as productive. But productive compared to what? Compared to the class of words it is defined to attach to. But this class is defined in terms of a nonuniversal rule feature, the feature + Latinate. If productivity can be defined with respect to such features, can any affix be less than 100 percent productive? The answer is not obvious.

We have so far drawn into question any firm conclusions based on differences in productivity among rules of morphology. What about differences in productivity between morphology and syntax? To illuminate this discussion, we will examine two subsystems of English verbs.

One subsystem is the Latinate subsystem, consisting of Latinate prefixes (*de-*, *in-*, *re-*, *sub-*, and so on) and stems (*-duct*, *-ject*, *-fer*, *-sist*); our discussion is based on Aronoff 1976:

	-ject	-sist	-fer	-duct
de-	*	*	*	*
in-	*	*	*	*
re-	*	*	*	—
sub-	*	*	—	*

As the chart reveals, this space of words is quite dense, at least for this (carefully chosen) sample. Does this mean that this morphology is productive? It is difficult to say, for two reasons. First, there are a finite number of Latinate prefixes and stems, so there are only so many possible forms of this kind, and most of them exist. Second, because there is no productive semantics for the class of forms, they must all be listed in any case. A good example is *subduct*—this word was probably invented in the service of the new theory of plate tectonics, and its meaning is technical and was invented simultaneously (similar to *subjacency* in linguistics).

We are not as interested in determining whether this system is productive as we are in comparing it with another system in English, the verb-particle system (*look up*) mentioned in section 1.1. This system is undoubtedly phrasal—a VP, with the head verb on the left: the left element takes inflection (*looks up*); the right element can be modified by adverbs (*look right up*); syntactic elements can intervenc (*look it up*); and so on. Consider the following array:

	give	throw	stand	look	call
up	*	*	*	*	*
down	—	.	.	.	*
in	*	.	*	*	*
out	*	*	*	*	*

Consider the similarities between this chart and the one of Latinate verbs. Again the space is dense—every form for these verbs and particles exists but one. Again there is no rule for giving the meaning of most of the forms ("*" designates noncompositional forms and "." compositional forms). And again the particles seem to be restricted to a subvocabulary—a particle with a Latinate verb is uncommon (**donate up*).

There seems to be no essential difference between the Latinate prefix-stem system and the verb-particle system with respect to either productivity or compositionality. But one of these systems is lexical and the other syntactic; that is, one is a part of the definition of English word, and the other is a part of the definition of English phrase. This suggests that it would be wrong to consider productivity as a criterial difference between syntax and morphology. There are both productive and unproductive phrase types and word types.

Of course some theoreticians have considered the verb-particle system to be lexical, and then we can draw no such conclusions. However, the only reason to consider this system to be lexical is in fact the lack of productivity and compositionality just considered. The system interests us precisely because it is formally phrasal and at the same time unproductive, which can be denied only at great cost—a jerrymandered definition of "word."

1.2.2 Blocking

The very curious phenomenon of "blocking" is also taken to be characteristic of words but not of phrases, and this notion is intimately connected with that of "listedness," which we claim is not a property of words in particular.

It is quite unclear what blocking actually is. Aronoff, with whom the term originated, says (1976, 45):

We may assume that the lexicon is arranged according to stems, and that for each stem there is a slot for each canonical meaning, where "canonical" means derived by regular rules. . . . Let us furthermore assume that for each stem there cannot be more than one item in each meaning slot."

So, for example, *gloriosity does not exist because gloriousness does; *graciosity does not exist because of graciousness; and so on (p. 44, (7)). In some cases both are permitted: curiousness, curiosity. Apparently the -ness forms are never blocked, whereas the -ity forms are. Aronoff accounts for this by saying that the -ness forms are not listed, the -ity forms are listed, and only listed forms are blocked.

There are several problems with this account. First, if unlisted, the -ness forms should neither be blocked, nor should they block, because they do not occupy slots in the lexicon. Or, if unlisted items are permitted to block, they should block uniformly and thus prevent any occurrences of -ity at all. Second, the asymmetry between -ness and -ity is accounted for in terms of a productivity difference, but again it is unclear that there is any difference—with X-ic forms -ity is 100 percent productive. Finally, the account of blocking given here is not sufficiently general in several respects that we will discuss shortly.

An important insight of Aronoff's is that blocking is based on meaning; for example, unbutton does not block rebutton because these differ in meaning. A word is blocked only by the existence of a synonym. A poll of speakers will doubtless reveal differences in meaning between *curiosity* and *curiousness* and all the other cases where dual forms exist. Actually, though, the mechanism involved may be a good deal more general than this: it may be that synonyms in general are blocked. Whenever two words mean the same thing, even where they are morphologically unrelated, they tend to diverge in meaning. A good example occurs in the terminology of linguistics—*argument* and *θ-role* were synonymous when the term *θ-role* was introduced. But it is now quite common to find these two terms used in different ways. We believe that this, like blocking, results from a general abhorrence of synonymy.

So far we have considered only blocking of words by words. Does any blocking involve phrases? Yes, although only in special circumstances. Obviously, synonymous sentences do not block each other, and it is difficult to say exactly what the domain of blocking is in syntax, just as it is in morphology. Nevertheless, blocking occurs in a number of cases in syntax, and in some cases blocking occurs across the syntax/morphology boundary.

A simple but striking case is the English comparative formation rule. Actually there are two such rules. One rule adds the suffix *-er* to monosyllables or disyllables ending in *-y*:

(6) hot → hotter; happy → happier
     *colorful → colorfuller

The other rule adjoins the adverb *more* to the adjective:

(7) more colorful

Interestingly, the second rule cannot apply to the forms that the first rule can apply to:

(8) *more hot

Clearly we want to say that the second rule is blocked by the first.[1]

---

1. Examples like (i)

(i) It is more hot than humid

do not refute the blocking proposal, since *-er* is impossible here:

(ii) *It is hotter than humid

And in fact *more* is not joined to *hot* here:

(iii) It is hot more than humid

Where *more* must be joined with the adjective, as in preverbal position, it is blocked where *-er* is possible:

(iv) *It is a more hot day

The feature of this system relevant to our discussion is that the first rule is morphological, and the second rule is syntactic. This means that blocking is characteristic, not of words in particular, but potentially of any kind of unit.

Of course we might formulate the rule for the syntactic adjunction of *more* in such a way that examples like those in (8) cannot be generated:

(9) Attach *more* to adjectives with two or more syllables, unless the last syllable is -*y*.

Then it will be unnecessary to appeal directly to blocking to account for (8). However, we must appeal to blocking to account for the peculiar relation that holds between the two rules—they are mutually exclusive. So blocking is still a phenomenon that does not regard the syntax/morphology boundary.

The reason that the two rules are in a blocking relationship clearly has something to do with the fact that the forms they produce have the same meaning and the same function, but this is just what we supposed for the case of purely morphological blocking.

A similar case involves the possessive constructions in English; some of them are formed by a syntactic adjunction (as in (10a)) and others by a morphological process (as in (10b)); the morphological process blocks the syntactic adjunction (as in (10c)):

(10) a. [the man I was talking to]$_{NP}$'s hat
  b. their hat
  c. *[them]$_{NP}$'s hat

Again, blocking between a morphological and a syntactic process must be appealed to. Another example of this, supplied by Aronoff in a personal communication, is the blocking of *the day after today* by the word *yesterday*.

We might appeal to blocking within syntax proper to explain why certain syntactic alternations are accompanied by a (sometimes subtle) difference of meaning or why certain constructions do not exist. For example, adjectives without complements rarely appear postnominally:

(11) a. the tall man
  b. *the man tall

However, when they do, they differ in meaning from prenominal adjectives in that they must denote "temporary" qualities (see Milsark 1974):

(12) John saw some people sick/*tall

We might reasonably associate this difference in meaning with blocking—if the pre- and postnominal positions had the same meaning, one would block the other, but a difference in meaning blocks the blocking.

Interestingly, when the adjective has a complement, the difference in meaning associated with the two positions disappears:

(13) The people as tall as Fred are here

This is because there are no longer two alternative positions for this complement, because the prenominal position is independently ungrammatical:

(14) *The tall as Fred people are here

This last fact strongly supports the idea that blocking is involved, for the difference in meaning disappears exactly when there are not two syntactic possibilities.

Other syntactic cases of blocking, which we will not detail here, include the following:

(15) a. The difference in meaning between instrumental and noninstrumental postcopular NPs in Russian
   b. The Avoid PRO rule proposed by Chomsky (1981)
   c. Reinhart's (1983) rendition of Principle C of the binding theory
   d. Chomsky and Lasnik's (1977) Biuniqueness Principle
   e. The *a/an* article alternation
   f. Montalbetti's (1984) condition on null pronouns

If any of these are actually due to some kind of blocking, then our conclusion that there is no special relation between blocking and morphology follows.

It remains a mystery what blocking actually is, and it is quite unclear under what circumstances it obtains. One of the clearest cases is the inflectional paradigm—speakers will not tolerate the idea that there might be more than one way to realize a certain inflectional form for a given verb. It is unclear whether some notion of paradigm will extend to the other cases of blocking, but it is worth nothing that even the core notion of inflectional paradigm cannot be restricted to words but must also include phrases. This is because languages contain both lexical and phrasal entries in their paradigms. The Latin passive, for example, is lexical for certain tenses but periphrastic, or phrasal, for others:

(16) | | Present | Perfect |
| --- | --- | --- |
| Active | amo | amavi |
| Passive | amor | amatus est |

If we left the phrasal passive out of this subparadigm, we would break its symmetry. So the notion of paradigm itself is not particular to the idea of word.

We have shown that blocking is not a phenomenon restricted to "words," though its exact applicability remains unclear. It may or may not have something to do with the notion of listedness. Despite current ignorance, we may at least conclude that the phenomenon itself cannot be used to support any thesis implicating listedness as an essential feature of the concept "word," because whatever blocking is, it is not restricted to words and in fact operates across the word/phrase boundary.

1.2.3   Why Words Are More Often Listed Than Phrases

So far we have not accounted for the widespread perception that listedness is a criterial property of words. This perception is not limited to and did not originate with linguists. Why does it exist? The perception is based on the fact that words are listed more often than phrases. But why should this be?

We feel that this difference between words and phrases flows simply from the fact that phrases are composed of words but not the reverse. Thus in a hierarchy of units phrases are "bigger" than words.

Why must some unit be listed? Morphemes must be listed because that is the only way to know what the morphemes are. But why must some larger unit, a composed word or phrase, be listed? Because it has a meaning or some other feature that does not follow from its composition. Why should there be such things? A listeme is generally a short encoding of a complicated but quite specific idea. Language users need short expressions for complicated ideas.

Linguistic theory defines a hierarchy of units where each unit is defined in terms of the previous one:

(17) morpheme > word > compound > phrase > sentence

This hierarchy is also a hierarchy of listedness:

(18) All the morphemes are listed.
     "Most" of the words are listed.
     Many of the compounds are listed.
     Some of the phrases are listed.
     Four or five of the sentences are listed.

Given the function of listing special forms, that of coding big things in small packages, it is not surprise that listing should be more common in the earlier members of the hierarchy than in the later ones. But notice that there is no special line to draw in this hierarchy, where listedness is characteristic of the units on the left but not of the units on the right. Further, consider the distinction between roots and stems, in the sense of Selkirk (1981), where stems (such as *complete*, *reject*) are composed of roots (*-plete*, *-ject*) but not vice versa. That roots are more often listed than stems is then a specific instance of the general functional explanation given above.

Perhaps the division of labor between words and phrases peculiar to English and the other Indo-European languages has misled linguists to regard listedness as a criterial property of word. In highly agglutinative languages it is inconceivable that every lexical item could be listed. Passamaquoddy, for example, has more than 10,000 forms for every verb (P. Lesourde, personal communication). The use of forms never heard before could well be the rule rather than the exception in such a language.

1.3 The Psychological Lexicon

We have suggested that the lexicon has no structure that corresponds to the structure of words assigned by word formation rules and that the listed/unlisted distinction itself corresponds to no lines that can be drawn by means of grammar or grammatical principle.

Still, speakers store words and phrases and retrieve them from this storage. In this section we will review some studies of this storage and retrieval, with a special eye to whether the posited storage and retrieval mechanisms observe distinctions made by formal grammar. If they do, then we must back away from our claim that the lexicon is not organized according to formal grammatical principles.

A good example is the study by Bradley (1980), whose results apparently suggest that there is a difference in the manner of listing items, depending on whether those items contain a morpheme boundary (+) or a word boundary.

Bradley's experiment is based on the frequency effect—a word is retrieved more rapidly from the lexicon if it is frequently used. She reasons that if a set of related words were all listed in the same lexical entry, then the frequency of that cluster of words (F_c) would govern the retrieval time, but if the words were listed separately, then the frequency of each word (F_p) would govern the retrieval time.

She found that for several word boundary affixes (namely, *-ment*, *-ness*, and *-er*), F_c governed retrieval, whereas for the morpheme boundary suffix *-ion*, F_p governed retrieval. This suggests that words derived by word boundary affixation are listed in the same lexical entry as the words they are derived from, whereas words derived by morpheme boundary affixation are listed as separate words.

Although this is compatible with our conclusion that membership in the lexicon does not correspond to any grammatical property, it is still not in the spirit of our view of the lexicon: items in the lexicon receive differential treatment according to their formal grammatical status. Is there an alternative view of Bradley's results that does not lead to this conclusion?

Bradley herself actually suggests the alternative: that the relative "transparency" of word boundary affixation, as opposed to morpheme boundary affixation, governs the storage process—the stem occurs relatively more "intact" in the former than in the latter. As Siegel (1974) has shown, in English word boundary affixation does not lead to stress shift, whereas morpheme boundary affixation does (*dictate, dictation*), and in a number of other ways morpheme boundary affixes mutilate the stem (*conclude, conclusion; destroy, destruction*) in ways that word boundary affixes do not.

It may then be that the relative transparency of the stem in the word determines whether F_c or F_p governs retrieval, where this transparency can be measured without reference to the boundaries involved and without reference to the rules that have applied to derive the forms. If this is so, then Bradley has demonstrated a principle by which the lexicon is organized for purposes of retrieval but not a principle derived from the grammar. A refutation of the view put forward here would involve showing that the boundary itself, independent of the degree of transparency of the derived items, determined how frequency was affecting retrieval times. The cases reported by Bradley will not support such a claim, and we know of no study that does. In conclusion there is still no reason to think that any grammatically defined class of object (root, stem, word, and so on) has any privileged, principled relation to the lexicon.

In a vein similar to that of the Bradley study, Stanners et al. (1979) seek to show that items derived by inflectional morphology are listed differently in the lexicon from items derived by derivational morphology. Their experiment is based on the "priming" effect: exposure to one word facilitates the retrieval of a later word if the two words are related, the more so the more related.

They found that exposure to a word formed by adding a regular inflectional ending facilitated later retrieval of the stem just as much as exposure to the stem itself would, whereas with a derivational ending the facilitation was weaker. They conclude that regular inflectionally derived words are stored with the stem, whereas derivationally derived words are stored as separate words.

In light of our position (in chapter 2, and in section 3.8) and that of Williams (1978)—that in morphology there is no difference between derivation and inflection—this is an unexpected result. Do the reported results show what they are meant to show, or is there another interpretation?

Stanners et al. control for the "transparency" phenomenon only to the extent that derivational morphemes that induce a small or no spelling change are singled out for special scrutiny (p. 408), and among them the priming effect is not full; so differences in transparency apparently do not play a role in determining differences in priming. However, the study does not control for stem changes other than spelling, and some of these changes, such as stress shift with *-ion* words, are arguably more relevent for retrieval, even for visually presented material. Futher, the derivational suffixes used are relatively less frequent ones (*-ion*, *-ance*, *-ence*) compared to some others, such as *-ness*. It is quite plausible to suppose that high-frequency suffixes affect storage and retrieval differently than low-frequency suffixes, regardless of whether they are derivational or inflectional, and that this is what the tests of Stanners et al. are tapping. In fact some of their own data support this idea, as relatively less productive inflectional morphology evidenced diminished priming, like the derivational cases and unlike the more productive inflectional cases. The most general conclusion that can be drawn from their work is that highly regular and productive (and perhaps transparent) morphology gives full priming, whereas less productive morphology gives diminished priming, though such a conclusion gives no privileged status to the derivational or the inflectional per se. Clearly the lexicon is structured to meet quite practical ends; the frequency and priming effects both illustrate this. One would like to know, What would be the advantage to the speaker in structuring the psychological lexicon by the structure induced by the rules of formation?

One argument often given for positing a privileged relation between the lexicon and the notion "word" is that speakers can tell the difference between an "actual" word and a potential (morphologically complex) word. How could this be, unless the speaker listed all words, as Jackendoff (1975) and Aronoff (1976) both presume? By contrast, speakers do not distinguish "actual" from "potential" phrases in syntax—thus it is reasonable to suppose that phrases are not listed. Thus we seem to have a principled basis for associating the notion "word" with the lexicon while still allowing listed phrases (idioms).

But there may not be a principled division to draw between words and phrases that has to do with the "actual" and the "potential." Rather we might try to explicate speakers' intuitions about this in terms of the hierarchy of units discussed in section 1.2.3:

(19) morpheme > word > compound > phrase > sentence

The hierarchy is ordered by the "composes" relation (morphemes compose words and so on) and has nothing to do with the categories given by the rules of formation; in particular there is nothing significant about the point in the hierarchy where we pass from compounds to phrases (the word/ phrase boundary). The explication of the intuitions about actual/potential would then be this: speakers have an extreme intuition about actual versus potential morphemes; they have a strong intuition about actual and potential words, and finer distinctions can be made with root and stem (root > stem); they have a weak intuition about actual versus potential compounds; they have little intuition about actual versus potential phrases; and they have no sense of a difference between actual and potential sentences.

There is some evidence that this view is correct. First, for English compounding (*China report*) there is little reason to draw the distinction between actual and potential; such compounds can be coined as freely as phrases in running speech, with neither speaker nor hearer taking special note of any transpiring linguistic novelty. Second, Aronoff (1983) reports a series of experiments demonstrating that the more productive a vein of morphology, the less likely that a speaker will be able to distinguish actual from potential words: "Speakers tend to judge potential words as actual words, though they are not" (p. 166). Thus the actual versus potential intuitions seem to register the productivity of the pattern and are not a useful criterion for wordhood.

If this is true, one would expect to find actual versus potential intuitions for phrases, though of course these would be weaker than intuitions for words, which are weak enough as it is. Nevertheless, some veins of phrase formation evidence the kind of limited productivity that gives rise to an intuition of actual versus potential. For example, the verb-particle construction, which is formally phrasal (it is syntactically transparent and has a leftmost head), shows this kind of limited productivity. Thus *crap off*, formed by analogy with *fuck off* and *screw off*, strikes speakers as a coinage rather than a freely formed phrase.

Thus we see from both ends that the actual versus potential intuitions concern the unit hierarchy, not any principled difference between words and phrases or any privileged relation of the word to the lexicon or listedness. This is consonant with the conclusions we have reached earlier in this chapter—effects connected with listedness (blocking, lack of productivity, and now the intuitions of actual versus potential) reflect the hierarchy of units from morpheme to sentence, not a binary distinction between word and phrase.

Given this, one might conclude that there is no binary distinction between word and phrase—that there is nothing more than the hierarchy of units. But we strongly disagree with this conclusion. There is a binary distinction to draw in the hierarchy of units—with morphemes, roots, stems, words, and compounds on one side (the words) and phrases and sentences on the other (the phrases). There are two bases for this distinction. One is the rules of formation; the rules of formation for words are a coherent whole, and the rules of formation for phrases are another coherent whole. For example, all words (in the present sense) are right-headed. (We will treat the nature of the rules of word formation in chapter 2.) The second basis for distinguishing words from phrases is the syntactic atomicity of words (treated in chapter 3). Words are opaque to syntactic descriptions and operations, but phrases are not. What gives us great confidence in concluding that there is a binary word/phrase distinction is that these two criteria coincide—what is formally a word (in the sense of chapter 2) is syntactically opaque (in the sense of chapter 3).

Under a number of views of morphology, such as the view of Aronoff (1976), the actual/potential distinction plays a crucial grammatical role that it does not play in our account. In Aronoff's account word formation rules themselves define this distinction—words generated by word formation rules are potential words, whereas all actual words are listed. As should be clear by now, the lexicon (as the list of actual words) can have no such status under our view. In most descendants of Aronoff's view, such as that of Lieber (1980), the actual words, along with the morphemes, are the sole input to the word formation rules.

This is not as innocuous as it sounds, at least on a strict interpretation. It means that the input to every word formation rule is an actual word, so every derived word is at most one remove from an actual word. This is a much more stringent restriction on derived words than simply requiring that they have a derivation (surely the minimal requirement)—under the stricter view every stage of every derivation must be an actual word.

To take a concrete case, consider the derivation of a complex word such as *unclearness*; is it derived "directly" from *unclear* as in (20a), or is it derived from *un-*, *clear*, and *-ness*, as in (20b)?

(20) a.

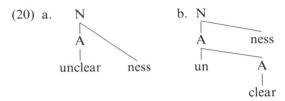

Of course one could regard (20b) as simply an abbreviation of two derivations under (20a); the real empirical content of the difference between the two views is whether the status as "actual" of the intermediate word (*clearness*) determines whether the derivation is well formed. Aronoff emphatically says that it does, which is what he means by his slogan "Words are formed from words"; and most have followed him, at least implicitly.

We reject this view because it makes the operation of the grammatical definitions contingent on the psychological lexicon. There are potential arguments against our view, and to maintain it we must explain why words that are "related" morphologically are also related in meaning. Under Aronoff's view *unclear* is related to *unclearness* because a word formation rule derives the latter from the former. Under our view, however, the latter is derived from *un-*, *clear*, and *-ness* and is not derived directly from *clearness*. Obviously, for this case there is no difference in predictions; under our view, because this is a compositional case, the meaning of *unclear* will come out the same whether derived on its own or as part of a larger structure, so the two will be related in meaning.

The more interesting cases are ones that are not compositional. For example, consider *pluralist* and *pluralistic*. Here *pluralist* has a meaning that is not derivable from *plural* and *-ist*, so let us say that this word is stored in the lexicon with its meaning. What might challenge our view is that *pluralistic* has this same element of meaning. We might conclude from this that *pluralistic* is derived from *pluralist* because the derivation would preserve the unpredictable element of meaning, but we disallow this kind of derivation because it makes the grammar of words contingent on the actual/potential distinction of the psychological lexicon.

Is there any other way to account for the relation between *plural* and *pluralistic*? Before considering that question, we will consider data from Williams 1981 suggesting that derivation is not the way to account for these meaning relations in any case; that is, we will show that certain words are related in the way that *pluralist* and *pluralistic* are but cannot be derived from one another.

One such case is *pluralist* and *pluralism*. These are clearly related in meaning and contain an element of meaning not inherent in *plural*, *-ist*, or *-ism*. Neither word can be derived from the other, unless we allowed word formation rules to delete morphemes or replace one morpheme with another (see Aronoff 1976, for a proposal along these lines). It will not help to say that they are both derived from *plural*, for the underivable element of meaning is not associated with the element *plural*. So there must be some other means for expressing the relatedness of these two words independent of their derivation. Such a means, the formation of constellations of words, is proposed in Williams 1981 and taken up here in section 3.8. Now, however, we want to emphasize that whatever this mechanism is, if it handles cases like *pluralist* and *pluralism*, it is likely also to handle cases like *pluralist* and *pluralistic* and thereby make unnecessary the derivational account of the meaning relation that holds in the latter pair. But if this is so, then we are not compelled to believe that the list of "actual" words is the input to the word formation rules, and we may assume that the input is simply the morphemes.

The principal reason for our suspicion of the view we have just rejected is that it gives a privileged relation between the lexicon and the rules of morphology, a relation we have rejected in general. There are numerous examples that are incompatible with that view as well, examples where a complex word is actual but some of its complex parts are not. Roeper and Siegel 1978 is full of such examples, such as *church-goer* (but **goer*) and *sad-seeming* (but **seeming*).

We are in essence insisting that morphology is more like syntax than heretofore thought. Both of course have lists—the list of primes, which are the words in syntax and the morphemes in morphology. In syntax there is of course no further list of "actual" versus "potential" phrases; the whole theory is about potential objects, though some are in fact actual (*How are you, kick the bucket*). In our view morphology is a theory of potential objects in exactly the same sense.

Chapter 2
Morphological Objects: The Rules of Word Formation

In this chapter we will examine the formal properties of the formation of words and arrive at a definition of "morphological object." We will see that some concepts of syntax, principally the notion "head," play a role in morphology, but that a number of principles are exclusively morphological and that morphology as a whole is a coherent system distinct from syntax, with its own symmetries.

The theory outlined here draws heavily on our earlier work (principally Williams 1978, 1978a, 1979, 1981, and 1981a), revised in light of further work of our own and of others (principally Selkirk 1982).

The ideas retained from earlier work are these: the thesis that words have heads and that suffixes are generally the heads of their words (Williams 1978, 1978a, 1981a); the thesis that suffixes belong to lexical categories (Williams 1978a, 1981); the thesis that affixes have argument structures, as do lexical items (Williams 1978, 1978a); the notion "external argument" (Williams 1978, 1978a, 1979, 1981, 1981a); the denial of the inflectional/derivational distinction in morphology (Williams 1978a, 1981; Lapointe 1979); and the general constraint that affixes cannot be assigned properties or be treated by rules in ways different from stems, except that they must be bound (Williams 1978a, 1978b).

In each case some modification of these ideas will be required, and some new concepts will also play important parts.

In section 2.1 we will review the rules of affixation and the notion "head." Here the influence of Selkirk (1982) will be evident.

In section 2.2 we will investigate rules for deriving the argument structures of compounds and affixed words. Again, the influence of Selkirk and a number of others will be evident.

2.1 The Rules of Formation

2.1.1 Phrase Structure of Words and Heads of Words

The work mentioned above (especially Selkirk 1982) is based on the idea that word formation rules are phrase structure rules, that is, rules specifying the concatenation of formatives that compose various morphological classes of object. For example, we might have the following rules for English:

(1) a. stem → af stem
    b. stem → stem af
    c. word → af word
    d. word → word af
    e. word → stem
    f. word → word word

Although these rules can "eliminated" in favor of principles or slogans such as "Affix α," there is nevertheless sufficient variation in what veins of word formation various languages exploit to wonder whether there might not be some notion of "rule." For example, English has few compounds of the form V–N (*bartend* is one exception), whereas some languages, such as Algonquian and Iroquois, have completely general compounding of this type. Is this due to the presence in these languages (and the absence in English) of the rule V → N V? See Selkirk 1982 for a discussion of various gaps in the English word formation system.

The theories of Williams (1978a, 1981a) and Selkirk (1982) are based on the notion that words have heads, just as phrases in syntax do. The identifying feature of heads in both syntax and morphology is that the properties of the head are those of the whole; in general, there is complete agreement of features between the head and the whole.

In syntax the head of a phrase is identified as the item with one less bar level than the phrase (or simply as the lexical daughter of the phrase):

(2) $X^n \to \ldots YP \ldots X^{n-1} \ldots ZP \ldots$

The head in syntax can be identified by virtue of an intrinsic property—the number of bar levels. The head of a phrase is the only daughter of the phrase that is not a maximal projection.

In morphology, however, such an identification of the head is impossible; the daughters of a compound are not intrinsically distinct from one another:

(3)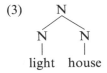

light   house

There is no way to know which is the head of this compound, because the two elements are both of the same level, namely, N.

Morphology avails itself of a different means of identifying the head of a word, a contextual means:

(4) The head of a word is the rightmost member of a word.

In compounds the role of the head is clear; it determines the category, plurality, and other general features of the word:

(5) [bar$_N$ tend$_V$]$_V$
     [apple$_N$ pie$_N$]$_N$
     [jet$_N$ black$_A$]$_A$
     [parts$_{PL}$ supplier$_{SG}$]   (singular)
     [part$_{SG}$ suppliers$_{PL}$]   (plural)

In each of these cases the rightmost element determines the category of the word, and in the last two cases this element also determines the plurality of the word.

The role of the head in compounding is the same as it is in syntax; in syntax the head determines the category and plurality of the phrase, among other things.

The notion of head and its identification as the rightmost element can be extended to words formed by affixation, as proposed by Williams (1978a). The affixation rules give us two structures, one for prefixes and one for suffixes:

(6)   word   word

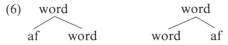

     af   word   word   af

The identification of head in morphology tells us that suffixes (but not prefixes) will be the heads of their words. This predicts that suffixes (but not prefixes) will determine the category, plurality, and so on, of their words, a prediction documented by Williams (1978a, 1981a). For example, the suffix -*ion* always derives nouns, but the prefix *counter-* (Williams 1978a) derives verbs (*counterscrew*), nouns (*counterspy*), and adjectives (*counterrevolutionary*), depending on the category of the word it attaches to.

How does a suffix determine the category of its word? Williams (1978a, 1981a) proposes that suffixes themselves belong to the categories N, V, and A, just as words do. There is no harm in regarding *-ion* as a "noun," so long as it is a bound form and thus cannot surface independent of a stem to which it is attached.

The notion "head of a word" allows for inflectional morphology to be reduced to derivational morphology. The principal mark of an inflectional affix is that it must appear outside derivational affixes; for example, the plural inflectional affix *-s* appears outside the derivational affix *-hood*:

(7) a. nounhoods
    b. *nounshood

It is not necessary to posit an extra level of morphology, either in morphology proper or in syntax, to account for this fact about inflectional morphology. Rather, it follows from the identification of heads in words. Inflectional morphemes are the ones that participate in syntax. This participation is greatly limited by the lexicalist hypothesis (see chapter 3), but one mode of participation remains: an affix may determine the properties of its word, and syntax may determine the distribution of words according to these properties. For an affix to determine the properties of its word, it must appear in the "ultimate" head position (the head of the head of the head ...), which explains why it must appear outside derivational affixes— if it appeared inside one of them, it would not be in head position.

In fact the real generalization about inflectional affixes is that they must appear in head position, not that they must appear "outside" all other word formation—the latter is partly a consequence of the former, although there are cases in which the former holds but the latter does not; for example, in (8) the plural appears "inside" the second element of the compound and yet determines the plurality of the entire compound because it appears in "ultimate" head position:

(8) N_{pl}
         ⟋‾‾‾‾⟍
      N N_{pl}
      | |
     wolf $children_{pl}$

2.1.2 Problems with the Notion "Head of a Word"

Several problems have accrued against the notion "head of a word," causing some researchers to restrict its applicability in various ways and others to reject it entirely. In this section we will review these problems and propose that instead of being rejected or restricted, the notion "head" should be relativized. The relativization capitalizes on the fact that heads in morphology (as opposed to syntax) are identified contextually.

First, Jaeggli (1980) observes that the diminutive suffix in Spanish can attach to almost any part of speech and that the resulting word belongs to the same category as the word to which the diminutive attaches:

(9) Adjective: poco   poquita
                  'little'
    Noun: chica   chiquita
                  'girl'
    Adverb: ahora   ahorita
                  'now'

This means that the diminutive does not determine the category of the derived word and so is not a likely head even though it occupies the rightmost position.

We feel that we can account for these facts and preserve the notion "head of a word" by relativizing the notion "head." Because the diminutive does not determine the category of the word to which it attaches, there is no reason (for the child or the linguist; see Williams 1980) to assign the diminutive to a lexical category; so the diminutive, like prefixes, is unspecified for category. Now, how can we get the category of the left member of these forms to determine the category of the whole? Suppose we define "head" as follows:

(10) Definition of "head$_F$" (read: head with respect to the feature F):
     The head$_F$ of a word is the rightmost element of the word marked for the feature F.

Because the left-hand elements of the forms in (9) are (by default) the rightmost elements of the forms marked for category specification, they are "head$_{category}$" (head with respect to category), and so the whole must agree with them in category.

The notion "relativized head" is peculiar to morphology (it has no analogue in syntax), and for good reason. In syntax the head is identifiable by an intrinsic feature (it is a nonmaximal projection), not contextually; so there can be no relativization of the head in syntax because there is only one potential head in the first place. The relativization of the head in morphology thus exploits the contextual definition of head in morphology.

The notion "relativized head" permits the possibility that words could have two heads, a head$_{F_1}$ and a head$_{F_2}$, where F_1 and F_2 are different features:

(11)

$$
\begin{array}{c}
\overset{\displaystyle X}{\overbrace{\qquad\qquad\qquad}} \\
\begin{array}{cc}
\quad Z \quad & \quad Y \quad \\
\left[\begin{array}{l} \text{unmarked} \\ \text{for } F_1 \\ -F_2 \end{array}\right] & \left[\begin{array}{l} +F_1 \\ +F_2 \end{array}\right]
\end{array}
\end{array}
$$

Here Y is the head$_{F_1}$ of X, and Z is the head$_{F_2}$.[2] There is nothing incoherent or disturbing about this situation, and in fact there are certainly cases of this kind.

Selkirk (1982) points out that Williams's (1981) explanation for the fact that inflectional affixes appear outside derivational affixes, which requires that inflectional affixes appear in head position, incorrectly entails that there can be only one inflectional affix per word. *Amabitur*, for example, is a Latin word with two inflectional affixes:

(12) ama   bi   tur
         + fut   + passive

She concludes (p. 77) that inflectional affixes cannot be heads, and she provides a means of passing up features that is independent of the notion "head."

We may instead suppose that *amabitur* has two heads, where *bi* is the head$_{future}$ and *tur* is the head$_{passive}$.

This account permits us to maintain that inflectional affixes are not separated from derivational morphology in any way; Selkirk's treatment accords them a special rule (p. 66) and percolation mechanisms not based on the notion "head" (p. 76).

Actually the peripherality of inflectional elements does not follow from the theory of relativized heads by itself. Suppose that alongside singular *boy* and plural *boys* there also existed unmarked *boy*, neither singular nor plural. Then in the following compound the plural on the left element, *choir*, could mark the entire compound as plural:

2. These definitions have empirical effects similar to those of Selkirk's (1982) and Lieber's (1980) percolation conventions and are actually responses to the same data that prompted their proposals, namely, the Spanish diminutives reported by Jaeggli (1980). Our proposal is conceptually quite distinct, however, because it preserves the role of "head" in determining the character of derived words, the same notion that is used in the computation of argument structures (in section 2.2); our proposal gives no special status to affixes and is thus consonant with our general view (and that of Williams 1978a) that affixes have no special properties (apart from having to be bound) that distinguish them from stems.

(13)   N_{pl}

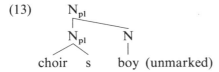

choir   s   boy (unmarked)

The problem is specific to the theory of relativized heads and did not arise under the theory of fixed heads in Williams (1978a, 1980).

To avoid this prediction, we must assume that all nouns are marked for number. In fact we must assume that all nominal elements are marked for number, in order to preserve the prediction in (7). And we must assume in general that if a feature is defined for a category, then all members of that category are marked for that feature.

Another instance of relativized head concerns argument structure and inflection. In general the argument structure of a form is determined by the argument structure of the head (which is not to say that it *is* necessarily the argument structure of the head; see sections 2.2 and 2.3 for proposals). However, for reasons already discussed, inflectional endings on verbs must appear in head position. So it would seem that a verb and the inflectional affix compete for head position, the former to determine the argument structure of the whole and the latter to pass up its inflectional features. Again, though, we may appeal to the notion "relativized head"— inflectional affixes are not marked with argument structures, so the head_{argument structure} will be the verb stem and not the inflectional affix, while the inflectional affix will still be the head_{inflectional features}:

(14)   V + sing, (A, Th)

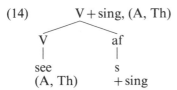

V   af

see   s
(A, Th)   + sing

In sum the notion "head$_F$" solves several different problems that have accrued against the idea that suffixes are heads of words and permits unified treatment of inflectional and derivational morphology (a distinction that we think is mythical in any case; see section 3.8). It exploits a possibility inherent in the fact that the head in morphology, as opposed to syntax, is identified contextually.

2.2   The Derivation of Argument Structures

In this section we will examine how the argument structures of complex words are derived, but before we begin, we will outline our assumptions, essentially those of Williams (1980, 1981a).

The argument structure of a predicate is a list of its θ-roles (Agent, Theme, Goal, and so on), with one of the arguments distinguished as the "external" argument, or θ-role (underlined in (15) and subsequent examples):

(15) see ($\underline{A}$, Th)

The external argument is the "head" of the argument structure. The rest are "internal" arguments, or θ-roles.

In syntax the internal θ-roles are assigned to constituents within the first projection of the predicate; essentially they are invisible beyond the first projection because the argument structure as a whole is not passed up the X-bar projection (see Williams 1979, 1984, and 1985 in particular). The assignment is marked by coindexation:

(16)

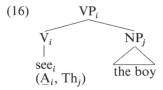

The external argument index is passed up the X-bar projection, as indicated in (16), because it is the head of the argument structure until it becomes a feature of the maximal projection of the predicate. It is then assigned to the subject of the predicate by the rule of predication, a species of θ-role assignment.

The key element of this system for our purposes is the distinction between the internal and external arguments. The argument structure as a whole does not "project" (perhaps because it is a complex of information, not a feature), so it is "available" only within the first projection. The index of the external argument does project, however, because it is the head of the argument structure and so is available outside the maximal projection, but it is the only such argument. There can only be one such argument because a node may bear only one index and there can be only one head.

2.2.1 The Derivation of the Argument Structure of Compounds

There has been much recent work on the derivation of the argument structure of compounds—see, for example, Roeper and Siegel 1978, Botha 1980, Allen 1978, Selkirk 1982, and Lieber 1983. We refer the reader especially to the detailed discussions in Roeper and Siegel. In this section we will examine the problem only in outline, with an eye to the relation of the notion "head of a word" to the problem of the derived argument structure of words.

The basic facts concerning the argument structure of compounds are these:

(17) a. A nonhead may but need not satisfy one of the arguments of the head.
    b. It cannot satisfy the external argument.
    c. The arguments of the nonhead are not part of the argument structure of the compound.
    d. Only the external argument of the head is part of the argument structure of the compound.

Example (18) illustrates (17a). A natural interpretation for (18a) is that the story is about destruction, whereas in (18b) the story is not about sobs—*sobs* does not satisfy an argument:

(18) a. destruction$_i$ story
       (R̲, A, Th) (R̲, A, Th$_i$)
    b. sob story

In neither of these does the head satisfy an argument of the nonhead. In fact there is a third possibility, unavailable in English (which we discuss in section 3.6.3)—the nonhead may not satisfy an argument but may restrict it in some way.

Example (19) illustrates (17b)—in this ungrammatical compound verb the external argument has been satisfied by the nonhead member of the compound:

(19) It was *boy-slept

(Because the compound would have no external argument, an expletive subject has been supplied.)

The failure of the nonhead to contribute any arguments to the argument structure of the compound (see (17c)) is illustrated by the ungrammatical (20):

(20) the *destruction-story of the city
    (meaning: the story of the destruction of the city)

Here the Theme argument of *destruction* does not become an argument of the compound as a whole and so is not available to be satisfied in syntax.

Finally, (17d) is illustrated in (21) (from Selkirk 1982, 36):

(21) *tree-eating of pasta

Here the nonexternal Theme argument of the compound does not become an argument and so cannot be satisfied in syntax. However, the external arguments of compounds are generally available; for example, in the verbal compound *bartend* the external Agent argument of *tend* can be satisfied in syntax:

(22) John$_i$ bar$_j$ tends

$$(\underline{A}_i, Th_j)$$

What is the explanation of these properties? Much of it is already accounted for by the principles governing the projection of argument structures.

As for (17a), perhaps we must stipulate that the "argument of" relation can hold between the nonhead and the head as one possible relation that can hold between members of a compound. It cannot satisfy the external argument, (17b), because that argument must pass its index up the X-bar projection to the maximal projection, and satisfying the external argument within the maximal projection would lead to a contradiction: the maximal projection would bear an index indicating that it contained an unsatisfied argument, but that argument would in fact be satisfied. Fact (17c) follows because the nonhead passes nothing to the whole, and (17d) follows from the fact that the external argument passes up the X-bar projection, but the argument structure as a whole does not, as discussed earlier:

(23) V_i

bar$_j$ tend$_i$

$$(\underline{A}_i, Th_j)$$

So the broad outline of the problem's solution already lies in what we have said about argument structure, and in particular what we have said about the difference between internal and external arguments.

Selkirk (1982), who observes facts relevant to (17b, d), accounts for them by means of the following pair of principles:

(24) a. The SUBJ argument of a lexical item may not be satisfied in compound structure. (p. 34)

  b. the First Order Projection Condition (FOPC): All non-SUBJ arguments of a lexical category X_i must be satisfied within the first order projection of X_i. (p. 37)

The problem with this formulation is that it is stated in terms of SUBJ, not external argument (in fact Selkirk argues explicitly that "external argument" is not the appropriate notion for the statement of these principles— see Williams 1984a for a critique of her argument). It therefore cannot avail itself of the rationale for the principles deriving from the different mechanisms for the assigning internal and external arguments and the relation of those mechanisms to the notion "head." In Selkirk's formulation the two principles having nothing to do with each other, and although the second is a generalization across syntactic structures and compounds, the first is particular to compounds. In our account all the facts in (17) derive from the fundamental properties of argument structure and θ-role assignment, properties laid out without reference to the properties of compounds in particular.

Some real empirical difficulties arise as well for Selkirk's principles, which again derive from the use of the notion "SUBJ" (see Williams 1984).

2.2.2 Affixes and Argument Structure

The basic principle operative in compounds also holds for the argument structure of words derived by affixation: the head determines the argument structure of the whole. But whereas the head of a compound relates to its nonhead by θ-role assignment, an affixal head relates to its nonhead not via θ-role assignment but via function composition. The latter is essentially the proposal made by Moortgat (1984).

2.2.2.1 Affixal Heads

As with compounds, the head of a word derived by affixation determines the external argument of the word. For example, the suffix *-ness* supplies an external argument to the word it is head of, and the external argument of the nonhead becomes an internal argument of the whole:

(25)

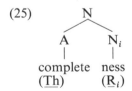

The external argument of *completeness* is the argument R that shows up in the paraphrase of the meaning of the word: the degree R to which such and such is "complete." So when *completeness* heads a referential NP, the NP refers to a degree of completeness, not to a thing that is complete. The external argument of *-ness* is the external argument of the whole, not the external argument of *complete*.

Similarly, the Japanese causative verbal suffix *-sase* bears an external argument, the causative Agent; that argument becomes the external argument of the whole, and the arguments of the nonhead verbal stem, including its external argument, become internal arguments of the whole (we illustrate with *tabe* 'eat'):

(26)
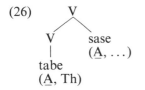

Finally, the verbal suffix *-ed* has no external argument (as proposed in Williams 1978); so the passive participle, which has this suffix as its head, also has no external argument (see Section 2.2.2.5), and the arguments of the nonhead stem are internal arguments of the participle:

(27)
```
        V
      /   \
    V       en
    |      (...)
   bite
  (A, Th)
```

In all three cases the affixal head determines the external argument of the whole; in the last case it determines that the whole will not have an external argument. (See section 2.2.2.5 for a somewhat different treatment of the passive.)

2.2.2.2 A Difference between Compounding and Affixation   Given the mechanisms that we have proposed so far, the external argument of the head must become the external argument of the whole in the examples of the preceding section. However, we would not expect that the external θ-role of *complete* in (25), for example, would become the internal θ-role of the whole. In fact, if affixation is like compounding, we would expect none of the arguments of the nonhead to be part of the argument structure of the whole.

Apparently an affixal head relates to its nonhead differently than the head of a compound does. The following form a minimal pair:

(28) a.   a baker of bread
       b.   *a bake-man of bread

Baker and *bake-man* mean roughly the same thing—'the one who bakes'. The first is formed by affixation and the second by compounding. The nonhead, *bake*, is the same in each. But only in the case of affixation does the argument of the nonhead (*bake*) become part of the argument structure of the whole word. We already have an explanation for (28b)—see section 2.2.1. But it remains to be explained why (28a) is possible.

2.2.2.3   θ-Role Satisfaction Versus Function Composition   Essentially the difference between compounding and affixation is this. In compounding the nonhead satisfies a θ-role of the head, in the familiar way. The nonhead of an affixal head, however, does not satisfy a θ-role of the affix; rather it "composes" with the affix—that is, the affix and the stem form a complex predicate.

To see the difference, let us first look at θ-role satisfaction again, in both syntax and compounding. Consider what it means for an NP to be assigned some θ-role T of predicate P. By the mechanisms discussed thus far and using the notation we have adopted, it means that the external θ-role of the head of NP will be coindexed with the θ-role T of P. For example, the verb *see*, which has two θ-roles, Agent for subject and Theme for object, and *owner*, which also has two θ-roles, the one who owns (external) and the thing owned (internal), will enter into the following structure when the latter is the object of the former:

(29)

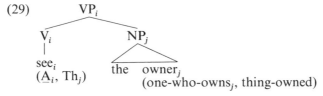

The coindexation of the Theme argument of *see* and the object is done by θ-role assignment; all other indexation is via projection. Because the Theme of *see* is coindexed with the external θ-role of *owner* (the "one-who-owns" argument), we know that the one-who-owns was seen, not the thing-seen.

The external θ-role of a noun whose maximal projection is used as an argument (for example, the one-who-owns argument of *owner* above) is not assigned to anything in the ordinary sense in which we think of θ-role assignment; rather it is "used up" by virtue of the fact that a θ-role is assigned to the NP. In such cases it is by virtue of the external θ-role that the NP can refer, when the NP is used referentially (*owner* refers to the one-who-owns, not the thing-owned). One interesting feature of θ-theory is that the argument assigned to a subject when an NP is used predicatively is the same one on which the reference of the NP turns when it is used referentially, namely, the external argument (see Williams 1981).

In compounding the mechanism for expressing the "argument of" relation is the same—some argument of the head is coindexed with the nonhead, yielding a representation in which it is coindexed with the external argument of the nonhead:

(30)

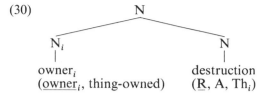

owner$_i$ destruction
(<u>owner</u>$_i$, thing-owned)   (<u>R</u>, A, Th$_i$)

Again, coindexation of the external argument of *owner* with the Theme argument of *destruction* is automatic once the Theme role has been assigned to *owner*, because the index of the external argument is part of the X-bar projection.

When an affixal head combines with a nonhead stem, the arguments of the nonhead stem, including the external argument, become part of the argument structure of the whole word. Importantly, the external argument of the nonhead is not used up as it is in θ-role satisfaction—it is still available and can be satisfied outside the word. Again consider the Japanese causative, for example:

(31) tabe   sase
     (<u>A</u>, Th)   (<u>A</u>)
     eat   make
     'make eat'

Although the Agent of *-sase* becomes the external argument of the whole word, as we expect, the external argument of *tabe* is not used up but is available and can be satisfied as an internal argument outside the word:

(32) John ga Mary$_i$ ni   tabe   sase
                          (A$_i$, ...)   (<u>A</u>)
     'John makes Mary eat'

Clearly *tabe* is not an argument of *-sase*, or its external argument would be used up by θ-role satisfaction.

We need another way for a head to relate to a nonhead, one analogous to "function composition." We will consider two ways to embed this relation in the system.

First, we might introduce a new kind of element into argument structures, an element abbreviated f (for *functor*) indicating that the item bearing that element in its argument structure is a "functor" with respect to a nonhead complement; we will then link this element with the nonhead complement with superscripts instead of subscripts:

(33) complete^i ness
     (<u>Th</u>)   (<u>R</u>, f^i)

We use superscripts instead of subscripts because the subscripts are used for the external argument, and the important thing about this relation is that it does not use up the external argument of the nonhead. Example (33) should interpreted as follows: first, -*ness* supplies the external argument of the entire word (the "degree" argument $\underline{R}$); second, -*ness* is a functor with respect to complete: the arguments of the predicate to which the head functor applies become arguments of the word as a whole.

Rather than introduce a new notation (f and superscripting), we might leave the argument structure unchanged and take the suffix to be a functor by virtue of its semantic type rather than virtue of some element in its argument structure:

(34) complete   ness   ⇒   completeness
      ($\underline{Th}$)   ($\underline{R}$)   ((Th)$\underline{R}$)
                    functor

We might then define the argument structure of derived words as follows:

(35) (The argument of the head) and the argument structure of the
       nonhead if the head is a functor

This second notation (or lack of it) for the functor relation embodies the hypothesis that functional composition and θ-role assignment differ in a fundamental way: although a verb may have several θ-roles, it may "compose" with only one item. In the previous notation it would be possible for the argument structure to contain two f's, f_1 and f_2, indicating that the form would compose with two different functions. As far as we know, there are no cases in which a functor must combine with more than one predicate.

Another point worth noting about (35) is that only the arguments of the nonhead become arguments of the head; adjunct modifiers of the nonhead do not become adjunct modifiers of the head, as (36) illustrates:

(36) the swimmer across the river

As pointed out to us by Tom Roeper, this can only mean 'the swimmer who is across the river', parallel to 'the man across the river'; it cannot mean 'the one who swims across the river'. In the latter *across the river* is interpreted as an adjunct modifier of the nonhead, and there is no mechanism for the adjunct modifiers of the word as whole to be interpreted as adjunct modifiers of the nonhead.

A further deficit of the f notation can be demonstrated only in syntax, because relevant cases do not exist in morphology.

Function composition occurs in syntax as well as in morphology. Consider the analysis of *John seems sick* given by Williams (1980, 1985):

(37)

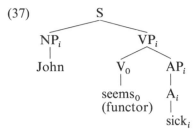

Here *seems* is a type 0 predicate, indicating that it takes no external argument. The external argument of the AP *sick* is "vertically bound" by the containing VP and ultimately assigned to *John*. But what is the relation between *seems* and *sick*? If *seems* takes *sick* as an argument, the external θ-role of *sick* will be used up and cannot be vertically bound and assigned to *John* without violating the Projection Principle. But suppose that *seems* is a functor—that is, the argument structure of *seems sick* is the argument structure of *sick*. Then the vertical binding is permitted because that is exactly what the vertical binding expresses. The argument structure of *sick* (the AP *sick*, not the lexical item *sick*) is one external argument; that argument is made an argument of the VP.

Small clause constructions of the *consider* or the *paint* type (as in *John painted the barn red*) may also be seen to involve composition. Suppose that *consider* is a functor with an external argument appearing in the following kind of configuration:

(38)

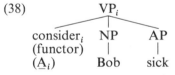

We might think of *consider* as combining with *sick* to compose a complex direct object-taking form, *consider-sick*. How does this combination take place? The AP *sick* has a single external argument; however, when it combines with *consider*, that external argument cannot become the external argument of *consider-sick* because *consider*, the head of the construction, already has an external argument, and the external argument of the head becomes the head of the whole. We might say that *consider* differs from *seems* above in that *consider* is head$_{\text{external argument}}$, because it has an external argument, whereas *seems* is not because it doesn't. Because the external argument of *sick* cannot become the external argument of *consider-sick*, it becomes an internal argument, which can be assigned to *Bob*.

This analysis captures the intuition of a number of linguists, including

Chomsky (1955) and Bach (1979), that *consider-sick* is a unit of some kind. What is important about the analysis here is that combining *consider* and *sick* is a syntax-level operation, not a lexical one, because it combines a word with a phrase (the AP *sick*). For this reason, only the external argument of the A *sick* plays a role in the combination.

Evidence for this analysis comes from the fact that in many instances there is selection between the verb and the predicate; *paint*, for example, can occur only with colors. And in many instances the predicate can occur adjacent to the verb even when the normal conditioning factors for Heavy NP Shift are absent (*wipe clean the slate*). This suggests that the verb and the predicate form some sort of unit apart from the object. This also solves a problem with the θ-Criterion for these examples; in essence the verb plus the AP assign a single θ-role to the complement NP.

The principal difference between the functors in syntax and morphology derives from the differences in the identification of head in the two systems. In syntax a head is the only nonmaximal projection in a phrase; so if the head is a functor, it is applied always to a one-place predicate, all maximal projections being one-place predicates. But in morphology a head functor may apply to *n*-place predicates, because the nonheads in morphology are not maximal projections.

We repeat that we know of no cases in which a head in syntax must apply as a functor to more than one nonhead, a possibility permitted by the *f* notation:

(39) verb

$(\underline{A}, f_1, f_2)$

This seems a good reason to reject this notation in favor of the system just outlined, in which the functor status of an item is not reflected in its argument structure.

A further reason to reject the *f* notation is that it permits the possibility of an "external" *f*:

(40) verb

$(\underline{f}, \dots)$

To our knowledge there are no cases in which a verb functionally composes with a predicate that is external to the projection of the verb.

A further instance of a functor in syntax is infl, which composes with the VP without saturating its external argument (see Williams 1985).

We have argued that the relation between a functor and the function that it composes with is fundamentally different from the relation between a predicate and the arguments it takes, and we have rejected extending the notation for arguments to functors. An affix (or a verb) is marked as a functor as part of the specification of its semantics.

We might consider going a step further and eliminating this marking altogether. This seems mistaken, however, in light of the following considerations. First, certain affixes do not seem to act like functors. For example, -ee, as opposed to -er, does not take over the arguments of the nonheads to which it is attached:

(41) a.   a libeler of Bill
     b. *a libelee by Bill

We may attribute this to the marking of -er as a functor and of -ee as not a functor (see more below).

The behavior of nominalizations without affixes also seems to support the view outlined here. These nominalizations (such as *hit*, *kick*, and so on) do not seem to support internal arguments (T. Roeper, personal communication):

(42) a. *the hit of Bill
     b. *the kick of Bill

Why is this? We believe that the answer lies in the fact that these nominalizations are headless, being derived by the rule (43) (a special instance of the rule given in Williams 1978a, 1981: X → Y):

(43) N → V

Clearly such a rule is headless because there is no agreement of features between N and V, so V cannot be the head of N. But if the rule is headless, then V is a (the) nonhead of N and thus cannot contribute anything to the argument structure of N—hence the ungrammaticality of the examples just cited.[3]

In this and the previous sections, we have assumed that affixation works strictly by function composition and that compounding works strictly by argument satisfaction. There is no reason for this, however; there is no reason why a stem marked as f could not serve as a function composer or an affix with an R ("referential") θ-role could not serve to satisfy an argument of the stem to which it was attached. An example in English of

---

3. One problem with this analysis is that it predicts that the N will have no external argument because there is no source for the external argument, which must come from the head. But of course the N does have an external argument; otherwise it could not head a referential NP. We are not sure what the answer to this problem is; perhaps there is a default assignment of external argument. It is worth noting that the external argument of the N is not the external argument of the V.

function composition in compounding might be a compound like *sad-seeming*; we already know that the *seem* is marked as a functor in syntax, and there is no reason to block this role for *seem* in morphology. A more extensive set of examples of function composition under compounding might be the serial verb constructions that occur in Haitian and many African languages and the composition of causatives in Romance languages (see section 4.2.2).

The opposite side of the coin, affixes that satisfy θ-roles, probably exists as well (see the discussion of Breton inflectional affixes in section 3.7).

What remains to be explained about English is why there is so little function composition in compounds (only *sad-seeming*) and why there is no argument satisfaction by affixes.

2.2.2.4 Control   So far we have considered mechanisms that determine the composition of the argument structure of derived words. However, morphology has certain means of specifying relations among arguments in an argument structure, which must also be accounted for. Consider, for example, the interpretation of the words formed by prefixing *self-* (discussed further in section 3.6).

(44) self   denial
         ($\underline{R}$, A_i, Th_i)

Here *self* not only satisfies the Theme θ-role but also binds it to the Agent θ-role.

A similar case is the Japanese suffix *-tai* 'want to'. Here *-tai* must be specified to be a functor, because the external argument of the nonhead stem is not used up by suffixation with *-tai* but is rather controlled by the external argument of *-tai*:

(45) tabe   tai
      ($\underline{A}$, Th)   ($\underline{A}$)
                    (functor)
      'eat'   Agent controls external argument of predicate

So, for example, *tabetai* has two arguments, the Agent of *-tai* and the Theme of *tabe*; the Agent of *tabe* is controlled:

(46) John$_i$ wa sushi o tabetai
              ((A_i, Th)$\underline{A}_i$)
      'John wants to eat sushi'

Control statements like the one on *-tai* also occur on full words and govern control in syntactic constructions:

(47) John performed the operation
     (A, Th)   (A, Th)
     Agent controls
     Agent of
     Theme

See Williams 1985a for discussion.

Finally, control must be invoked to explain the difference between -*er* and -*ee*. Both are functors, but -*er* specifies control of the external argument, and -*ee* specifies control of a nonexternal argument:

(48) a. employ   er
     (A, Th) (R)
           R controls external argument
           of the predicate
    b. employ   ee
     (A, Th) (R)
           R controls internal argument
           of the predicate

In each case the control relation satisfies the controlled argument so that it cannot be expressed in syntax independent of its controller.

2.2.2.5 Applications: Passive, Applicative, and Antipassive   In this section we will review several construction types to show how they can be treated under the proposals developed here. We will consider a solution adequate if we can determine the argument structures of composite forms from those of the component parts under the principles already outlined, and under the further stricture that affixes be assigned argument structures and features no different from those assigned to stems.

The (verbal) passive morpheme -*en* is treated by Williams (1978) as having no external argument; because it appears in head position and has no external argument, the resulting word has no external argument, the desired result, since the passive form has no external argument, by assumption. The external argument of the stem becomes internalized by convention and is realized in a *by*-phrase, which is the marker of the Agent θ-role.

This treatment must be somewhat modified in the present context. If the head of a word has no external argument but the nonhead does, then the external argument of the nonhead will become the external argument of the whole, because the nonhead will be head$_{\text{external argument}}$ under our conception of relativized head. This is because the index of the external argument percolates via the chain of heads. So giving the passive morpheme -*en* no external argument does not have the desired effect by itself.

The passive morpheme must be given some means of eliminating the external argument of the nonhead. A means already available for this is control, and the likely candidate for the controller is the *by*-phrase argument. So the passive morpheme will be assigned the following representation:

(49) V   en
    (A̲, Th, G)   (functor)
                     (X)
                     |
                     PP_{by}
            X controls external argument

Because -*en* is a functor, the arguments of the nonhead will be taken over as arguments of the whole; in addition the X argument of -*en* will be an argument of the whole because -*en* is the head$_{\text{argument structure}}$; the external argument of the nonhead does not become the external argument of the whole because it is controlled by the X (*by*-phrase) argument of the head; so the whole has no external argument.

The control of the external argument of the stem verb by the *by*-phrase argument of the passive morpheme yields the intuitive result that the *by*-phrase of the passive corresponds to the subject of the active. In fact this is an improvement over the previous account, in which the *by*-phrase was the realization of the internalized Agent, for as several linguists, including Jaeggli (1986), have pointed out, the *by*-phrase realizes whatever argument the subject of the verb is, whether or not it is an Agent; for example, with *know* the subject is an "Experiencer" or something like that, and the passive is possible nevertheless:

(50)   V ((Exp_i, Th) X_i)

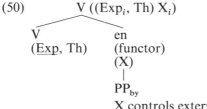

  V   en
  (Exp̲, Th)   (functor)
                  (X)
                  |
                  PP_{by}
          X controls external argument

The Experiencer is correctly assigned to the *by*-phrase, permitting the passive:

(51) The answer was known by Fred

In the passive nominal, which significantly does not involve morphology and consequently does not involve control, the *by*-phrase is restricted to

Agents:

(52) a. *knowledge of the answer by Fred
     b. delivery of the message by Fred

This is because the *by*-phrase truly does realize the internal θ-role Agent in nominals. There are then two sources for *by*—it is the realization of the X argument of the passive morpheme *-en*, and it is the realization of internal Agents. Because many passive verbs have internalized Agents, it is understandable that the two *by*'s would be confused, but the wider range of realizations for the *by* of the verbal passive shows that the two are distinct.

The applicative constructions are just like the passive except that there is no controller for the external argument of the stem. Thus the external argument of the stem becomes the external argument of the whole. We will illustrate with the applied affix of Chi-Mwi:ni, drawing on the discussions of Marantz (1985, 231f.) and Kisseberth and Abasheikh (1977).

The applied affix of Chi-Mwi:ni (*-il*) adds an extra accusatively marked internal argument to the verb it is joined with; the argument can be of various types, including Instrumental and Benefactive (illustrated in (53), from Marantz 1985, 231):

(53) a. Hamadi $\emptyset$-sh-pishile   cha:kuja
         Hamadi SP-OP-cook-T/A food
         'Hamadi cooked the food'
     b. Hamadi $\emptyset$-wa-pik-il-ile   wa:na   cha:kuja
         Hamadi SP-OP-cook-APPL-T/A children food
         'Hamadi cooked food for the children'

We may achieve this result by assigning the Chi-Mwi:ni affix *il* the following designations:

(54) -il: f (X)
            acc

Because *-il* is a functor, all the arguments of the stem will be carried over. In addition the argument X of *-il* will be an argument of the whole because *-il* is the head of the whole; further, the *-il* argument will be realized as accusative. Because the head has no external argument and because it does not control the external argument of the stem, the external argument of the nonhead will be the external argument of the whole, as the stem will be head$_{external\ argument}$; in this last respect the applied affix differs crucially from the passive morpheme *-en*. Example (55) illustrates all these properties:

(55)

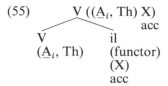

Note the crucial role played by the notion "head$_{external\ argument}$" here. The applied suffix is the head in some absolute sense, as it must be if it is a functor; however, it is not the head$_{external\ argument}$, and so the stem supplies the index of its external argument.

In an ergative language the subject of an intransitive is in the same case as the object of a transitive (the absolutive case), and the subject of a transitive is in the ergative case. In the antipassive construction a specially affixed transitive verb appears with its subject in the ergative and its object in an oblique case.

We may treat this as a case of control. We will illustrate with an example from Greenlandic Eskimo, as discussed by Woodbury (1977) and Marantz (1985):

(56) a. Anut-ip   miirqa-t   paar-ai
        man-ERG child-PL(ABS) take care of-IND-3sg3pl
        'The man takes care of the children'
     b. Anut-0   miirqu-nik   paar-si-vuq
        man-ABS children-INST take care of-ANTIPASS-IND3sg
        'The man takes care of the children'

Sentence (56b) is the antipassive of (56a). The question is, What assignment of argument structure of the ANTIPASS morpheme -*si* will give the desired result? Again, a rule of control does the trick:

(57) il
      (functor)
      (X)
      NP$_{INST}$

      X controls ABS argument

The instrumental case is assigned to X, which controls the absolutive argument of the stem.

When this affix is added to a verb, we get the following result:

(58)   V((A, Th) X)

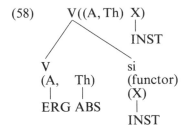

Here the absolutive Theme of the stem is not realizable in syntax because it is controlled in morphology by the X argument of the antipassive suffix. The Agent argument of the whole is marked absolutive, not ergative, because the whole will not otherwise have a realizable absolutive.

2.3   Conclusion

In this chapter we have discussed two calculi that enter into the determination of the properties of derived words. One has to do with the features of the derived word, and these are basically determined by the definition of head, relativized in the way we have outlined.

The other has to do with the calculation of argument structures of derived words in terms of the argument structures of the parts. Again, the argument structure of the whole is determined by the head. We examined two ways in which the head could be related to the nonhead—the nonhead can satisfy a θ-role of the head, as in compounding, or the head can functionally compose with the non-head, as in affixation.

Both calculi determine properties of wholes from properties of parts. It will be our thesis in chapter 3 that rules of syntax do not have access to the parts of words directly, only to the "topmost" properties of word: the features and argument structure of the topmost word.

Chapter 3

Syntactic Atoms:
The Syntactic Atomicity
of Words

In this chapter we turn to our thesis that the lexicalist hypothesis is not so much a thesis of grammar (like an island condition) as it is a statement about the global architecture of grammar: the theory of grammar has two subtheories, morphology and syntax, each with its own atoms, rules of formation, and so on.

We regard the need for the lexicalist hypothesis (especially the lexical integrity hypothesis) as arising from a fundamentally mistaken idea of what a grammar is. The hypothesis is true in that morphology and syntax are separate in the way that it says they are, but ideally it should "go without saying," just as the principle that separates history from forestry "goes without saying." Morphology and syntax are different (though similar) sciences about different objects, so the idea that the derivations in one could get mixed up with those of the other should not arise in the first place.

3.1 Syntactic Atom Versus Morphological Object

We might take the content of the notion "word" to be given by the notion "morphological object" just outlined—the words of a language are simply the morphological objects of the language. This at least embodies the insight (if it be) that "listed" is not criterial or even relevant. However, it can be shown that there is another notion of "word" empirically and conceptually distinct from the one just given—a notion we will call *syntactic atom*. The syntactic atoms are the primes of syntax.

One would of course hope that the syntactic atoms of a language would be exactly the morphological objects of the language, and ideally this is so. However, it can be shown that some properties of morphological objects hold of a set of items that properly includes the morphological objects;

principal among these properties is that of "syntactic atomicity," that is, the inability of syntactic rules to "analyze" the contents of X^0 categories. Syntactic atomicity is certainly a property of morphological objects, as is well known, and the explanation for a great many cases is trivial—syntactic rules simply lack the vocabulary for analyzing morphological objects—a vocabulary that would include *stem, affix, prefix,* and so on. We depart from a number of recent researchers in supposing that the vocabulary of syntax does not include these items—for example, Pesetsky (1985), Farmer (1980), Fabb (1984), Botha (1980), Borer (1984), Roeper (1987), Anderson (1982), and others. In these theories the syntactic vocabulary must have such terms as *affix,* and syntactic rules must be capable of attaching, moving, and otherwise analyzing affixes. There are undeniably observable interactions between morphemes and syntax; for example, the plural morphemes -*s* appears attached to the right of nouns heading NPs that are the subjects of VPs headed by plural Vs; however, we feel that the interactions are such that it is not necessary to intermix the terms and rules of syntax and morphology. Rather the two theories share a small theoretical vocabulary, including the parts of speech and certain features (such as "tensed"), and the interpenetration that exists is channeled through this shared vocabulary. In the next section we will outline how this very limited shared vocabulary can account for most interactions, or interpenetrations, of syntax and morphology in a way consistent with the syntactic atomicity of words.

Beyond this, however, we can show that the syntactic atomicity of words cannot be reduced to the (near) disjointness of the vocabularies of syntax and morphology, for in many cases the vocabulary of syntax contains the relevant terms for analyzing certain kinds of words, as we shall see, and yet it still is not possible. In chapter 4 we will discuss a class of objects that do not have morphological form but do display syntactic atomicity. Therefore, morphological form and syntactic atomicity are conceptually distinct and, as it turns out, not coextensive properties.

3.2   The Interface of Syntax and Morphology: The Shared Vocabulary

The theory of morphology outlined in chapter 2 allows us to say precisely how morphological material can register its effects in syntax. We have been referring to words as "atomic," but actually they are not atomic in two important ways. First, each word is classified according to various features, or properties, such as $\pm N$, $\pm V$, $\pm$plural, $\pm$noun-class 3, and so on.

Second, words have argument structures, which can be quite complex, consisting of perhaps several arguments, contextual and selectional restrictions on the arguments, binding of arguments by other arguments, and so on. Further, the (extended) categorial features and the argument structure constitute a shared vocabulary of the theory of morphology and the theory of syntax, and a means by which one theory may "communicate" with the other.

Rules of sentence-level syntax have access to both of these kinds of information. The base rules—of case assignment, agreement, and movement—have access to the categorial status of lexical items; rules of θ-role assignment and control have access to the argument structure of lexical items. Given this wealth of information, highly structured information in the case of argument structure, it is perhaps misleading to refer to words as syntactically atomic. We will continue to do so, however, for there is an important sense in which words are atomic: although syntactic rules can access the categorial status and argument structure of a lexical item, they will never depend on how that categorial status or argument structure was arrived at through morphological derivation or on the internal constituency of words. The rules of syntax can see that a word has such and such properties, but they cannot see how it came to have those properties.

Though syntax and morphology share some theoretical terms, such as the parts of speech, the terms concerning argument structure, and so forth, the vocabularies are distinct. We assume, for example, that syntax does not avail itself of the notion "affix"; if it did, our atomicity thesis would be in jeopardy. Perhaps a majority of theories of morphology permit the interpenetration that we think is impossible (for example, the works listed earlier in this chapter). In general these theories take grammar to be one big theory of "sentence," a theory that contains the theory of "word," and they consider syntax and morphology to be simply two components of this general theory of sentences.

Another way to understand the content of the atomicity thesis is to consider under what circumstances the categorial status or argument structure of an affix can play a role in the syntax of a sentence. The atomicity thesis says that the affix can register a syntactic effect only by affecting the categorial status or argument structure of a word in a sentence, and it can do this only by the rules of morphology as given in chapter 2.

For example, the plural marker *-s* affixed to a noun makes the NP projected from that noun plural and ultimately "agrees" with a plural VP:

(1)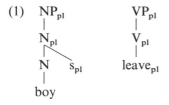

This participation of the affix in syntax is possible only because syntax and morphology share a vocabulary of features, such as ±plural and the features for the parts of speech.

Importantly, the rules of morphology, not those of syntax, determine whether an affix can register a syntactic effect in this way. In (2) (T. Roeper, personal communication) the plural marker does not make the containing NP plural, and this fact is determined by the rules of morphology:

(2)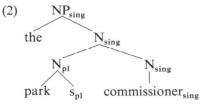

The rules of syntax cannot discriminate among compounds whose nonhead members are plural or singular, because the rules of morphology determine that only the features of the head become features of the word as a whole. The question of atomicity can be put this way: How can part of a word (such as an affix) interact with the syntactic (extramorphological) environment—what are the permissible ways? The most interesting answer is, only indirectly; it will first interact with the other parts of the word to determine the properties of that word, and that word will then interact with syntax (it will have a syntactic distribution).

3.3 Atomicity

Words are "atomic" at the level of phrasal syntax and phrasal semantics. The words have "features," or properties, but these features have no structure, and the relation of these features to the internal composition of the word cannot be relevant in syntax—this is the thesis of the atomicity of words, or the lexical integrity hypothesis, or the strong lexicalist hypothesis (as in Lapointe 1979), or a version of the lexicalist hypothesis of Chomsky (1970), Williams (1978, 1978a), and numerous others. In this section we will examine this property of atomicity and consider again why it holds.

First, words are "generic" in meaning in a way that phrases are not. It is difficult to put a finger on what this genericness amounts to, but it is nevertheless quite palpable and pervasive. For example, compare the word *robber* and the phrase *man who is robbing the bank*. One cannot say *John is a bank robber* to mean 'John is robbing a bank at this very moment'. *Robber* seems to denote a permanent property, whereas *is robbing a bank* is completely timely. All this must be qualified, of course—for example, in *That one time, John was the bank robber and Bill was the getaway man*, *robber* seems to denote a very temporary property.

What is the source of this difference? Perhaps it is that sentences contain references to time, via tense markings, whereas words contain no such references. Perhaps the absence of references to time gives the generic character to the meanings of words.

Why do words not contain time references? Perhaps it is because time references, to be interpreted, must be accessible to the rules of sentence interpretation. The atomicity of words prevents word-internal time references from being assigned time values in the way that "tense" is. Perhaps in general reference is associated only with maximal projections: NPs refer to objects, Infl' refers to time, Comp' refers to truth values.

Pronominal reference is not allowed in words either—thus, for example, we find no compounds of the form *it robber*, with *it* referring to some bank. In this case it is not trivial that the reference is blocked; we cannot appeal to the disjointness of the vocabularies of syntax and morphology, for syntax contains the category "pronoun," so it is unclear why pronominal reference cannot be assigned to the compound-contained pronoun. There are two possibilities. First, it may be that "reference" is assigned only to NPs, and internal to the compound we have only an N. Or it may be that the inside of X^0s is inaccessible to syntactic (or sentence-level semantic) rules, regardless of whether the syntactic rules have the vocabulary for "analyzing" words into parts. We will keep both possibilities in mind as we proceed, though it appears that the latter must be correct, whether or not the former is.

Finally, words are also "referential islands" for proper names: **Bill admirer*. Famous names seem to be an exception to this: *Nixon admirer*. However, in such expressions the name is not truly referential; this can be seen from the fact that (3a) is not contradictory and (3b) is:

(3) a.   John is a Nixon admirer in every sense except that he does not
          admire Nixon

b. *John admires Nixon in every sense except that he does not
   admire Nixon

c. *Who is John an [t admirer]

As before the compound denotes a generic property, and apparently even
the compositionally derived property *admires Nixon* is not an essential
component of the property denoted. As (3c) shows, a variable cannot be
substituted for a name in this context.

Syntactic atoms are also atomic with respect to surface filters. English
contains a Head-Final Filter on prenominal modifiers prohibiting them
from terminating in anything other than their heads. For example, consider (4):

(4) a.   the very proud man
    b.   *the proud of his children man
    c.   *[w X y]N $y \neq 0$

In (4b) [proud of his children] does not terminate in its head, *proud*, hence
the ungrammaticality of the phrase as a whole. Now consider (5):

(5) the [much talked about t] new show

Here we have a prenominal modifier that does not appear to end in its
head—the head would appear to be *talked*, but the phrase ends in *t*. This
counterexample may be deflected, however, if the non–head finality of the
phrase is word-internal—then the atomicity of words will prevent the filter
from detecting the non–head finality. This can be achieved if the phrase
talked about t can be assigned to the category A^0. Never mind now how
such an assignment can be made. With this assignment, this example has
the following structure:

(6) the [much [talked about t]$_A$]$_{AP}$ new show

Here the phrase *much talked about t* does end in its syntactic head, the A
talked about t; that the A does not end in its head is irrelevant to the
syntactic filter because the offense is internal to the word.

This example clearly shows that the atomicity of words cannot be
reduced to the (near) disjointness of the vocabularies of syntax and morphology because the internal structure of the phrase *talked about t* is clearly
syntactic. In the next section we will discuss why atomicity holds, because
it does not so reduce.

Is there any further reason for assigning the structure we have assigned
in (6)? Apparently there is. A consequence of the theory of atomicity to be
outlined in the next section is that if some collocation is syntactially atomic

in any sense, then it is so in all senses. Phrases like the one in (6) should exhibit other types of atomicity besides evasion of the Head-Final Filter. For example, they should not contain specific time or individual references, and the following examples seem to bear this out:

(7) a. *the much [listened to t by Fred]$_A$ music
    b. *the much [listened to t today]$_A$ music

To escape the filter the prenominal material must be bracketed as indicated in (7); so bracketed, though, the expressions are ill formed because the referential items *Fred* and *today* occur inside X^0. So the referential opacity of X^0 is a consequence of the syntactic (filter) opacity of X^0—in other words, *words are opaque to all sentence-level operations or descriptions*. This linking together of these two kinds of opacity gives the view outlined here its empirical teeth.

3.4 What Atomicity Holds of and Why

It is an important though seemingly trivial property that syntactic atomicity holds of all words and only of words. It is a far from necessary truth, for example, that compounds are atomic in exactly the same way that words formed by affixation are:

(8) a. *[How complete -ness] do you admire
    b. *The who-killer did the police catch

These show that words formed by affixation, as in (8a), as well as words formed by compounding, as in (8b), are both atomic with respect to the syntactic (or phrasal) rule of *Wh*-Movement.

It could easily have been otherwise; compounds, for example, could have been transparent to *wh*-syntax, whereas affixed words were atomic. Why are compounds like affixed words and not like phrases? One is tempted to view the units of language in a hierarchy (see chapter 1):

(9) Sentences, NPs and VPs, compounds, affixed words, stems, roots

From this point of view, we might say that syntactic atomicity held of everything below and including compounds. But the drawing of this line is arbitrary. It is especially so when one considers the similarities between compounds and phrases—we have seen, for example, that we find θ-role satisfaction in both, and there is even a generalization concerning θ-role assignment that covers both, the FOPC (see chapter 2):

(10) [see the dog]$_{VP}$
     [dog seer]$_N$

Compounds are grouped with words instead of phrases because compounds are formally similar to affixed words and formally dissimilar to phrases. In particular compounds are head-final, like affixed words, whereas phrases are not. Even the similarity of θ-role assignment just mentioned is misleading, because it is the one fixed relation allowed to hold between a verb and its object, whereas it is just one mechanism by which the two elements of a compound can be related—the root compounds (*dog sled*) are interpreted entirely differently, even though they are formally similar to the verbal compounds exhibiting θ-role assignment. This shows that compounds are in no way parasitic on syntax, even though there is some overlap of interpretive mechanisms.

So two unrelated ways of dividing up the universe of linguistic objects converge: those that share the formal property of being head-final share the further property of being syntactically opaque, and only those. We feel that this convergence gives the notion "word" its surest content.

One way to ensure the syntactic atomicity of words is to place the rule of "lexical insertion" after all the syntactic rules that could possibly analyze the interior constituents of words (in the sense of syntactic atoms); so lexical insertion could be at S-Structure, for instance.

The real content of such a proposal is subtler than it seems at first glance. What is not at issue, for example, is whether transformations and other operations and filters are sensitive to particular lexical items; they obviously are. So the question is, How does this sensitivity come about?

Suppose that lexical insertion takes place at S-Structure. Suppose that a transformation is sensitive to a particular class of lexical items, as *Wh*-Movement is—the *wh*-words. This sensitivity can be expressed even in a theory with surface lexical insertion: a "*wh*" feature can be assigned in the syntax to (empty) D-Structure nodes; the transformations will operate on structures so marked; and lexical insertion will insert *wh*-words in and only in $+wh$ nodes.

This is even true for transformations and filters sensitive to a single lexical item—the lexicon will have simply have one item in the class of items insertable for nodes marked with some particular feature.

With features, then, it would seem that the S-Structure hypothesis is almost indistinguishable from the D-Structure hypothesis. That is so except for one thing—the atomicity of words follows from the S-Structure hypothesis but not the D-Structure hypothesis because features have no structure. So even when a syntactical feature uniquely identifies a particular lexical item, it does not tell anything about the internal structure of the lexical item, so that information is not available.

Thus the two hypotheses are distinct. The S-Structure hypothesis is not obviously distinct from another theory of atomicity, the one embodied in Pesetsky's (1979) Bracket Erasure Convention. According to that view, words are inserted in D-Structure, but all the bracketing that indicates the words' internal structure, as assigned by the lexicon, has been erased. Rather than trying to dream up the recherché considerations that might distinguish these two views, we will present a third view, which we think answers some questions that neither S-Structure insertion nor the Bracket Erasure Convention can be squared with.

First, what is syntax about? We could say "sentences" in the usual sense, but another answer could be "sentence forms," where two sentences belong to the same sentence form if one can be derived from the other by substitution of one lexical item for another belonging to all the same syntactic classes. In other words syntactic forms are "wordless" phrase markers. "Sentence," then, as ordinarily understood, is not in the purview of syntax, although the syntactic forms that syntax *is* about certainly contribute to the description of "sentences."

This view is empirically difficult to distinguish from the S-Structure insertion theory, despite the fact that it pretends to view the question from a higher ground. Our preference for the "sentence form" view rests entirely on our feeling that the atomicity of words derives from something more fundamental than the theory-internal propositions that constitute the S-Structure insertion theory and the bracket erasure theory.

3.5 Pseudopassive

Hornstein and Weinberg (1981) observe, following Chomsky (1973), that the reanalyzed material of a passive must be a "natural predicate" in some sense. The view of atomicity just outlined will allow a sharper understanding of the term *natural predicate* and will also explain why this condition holds for pseudopassive constructions but not for preposition stranding by *Wh*-Movement.

As for what the term *natural predicate* means in this context, it really comes down to the genericness and referential opacity of X^0 already discussed (section 3.3). So, for the example, the pseudopassive cannot incorporate a referential expression:

(11) *Bill was [sent some books to]$_V$ t

We may therefore expect exactly the same sense of the term *natural predicate* to hold here as held in the case of the prenominal filter exceptions and as will hold in the discussion of the French causative construction (to follow).

Certain exceptions to this opacity are found, as, for example, in (12):

(12) John was [taken advantage of]$_V$ t

We might appeal here, as does Fiengo (1974) to the claim that *advantage* does not have full referential value in this construction, thus being an exception that (nonparadoxically) proves the rule. This can be supported by such examples as those in (13):

(13) a. *Bill was [taken great advantage of]$_V$
      b. *How much advantage was Bill [taken t of]$_V$ t

Although the notion "natural predicate" remains murky, at least several cases are now linked together (prenominal modifiers, pseudopassive, and French causative, not to mention ordinary words), so the possibilities are somewhat narrowed. But the problem of greatest interest in the context of the theory outlined here is why the pseudopassive is subject to this condition whereas the stranding of Ps by *Wh*-Movement is not:

(14) Who did John give some books to t

The reason for this difference follows directly from the view of opacity we have outlined.

Passivization involves two lexical operations—the retraction of θ-assignment to the subject and the retraction of case assignment to the object. If case were not retracted in this way, the passive structure would be ungrammatical, for a case-marked trace (in object position) would be A-bound (by the subject). Nothing else said, all the examples where NP-Movement has moved the object of a preposition should be ungrammatical, because the preposition will assign case to its (A-bound) object. However, Reanalysis, which assigns the preposition to the interior of a word (or X^0), can be used to avoid this type of ungrammaticality, because the resultant word can undergo the lexical operation of case retraction, and, further, the preposition, occurring inside the resultant word, cannot assign its case because of the atomicity of X^0. In short, to avoid assigning its case to an A-bound trace, a preposition must be reanalyzed as part of a word— nothing else will do. But, then, of course, the "predicate" condition follows automatically because it is a condition on all words.

Wh-preposition stranding involves no such condition, for the simple reason that *wh*-trace can (in fact must) be case-marked, so the case-assigning preposition can (and in fact must) remain accessible to syntactic rule.

In this account of the difference between *wh*-preposition stranding and pseudopassive we have again relied on the dictum "Opaque for one purpose, opaque for all purposes," in that we have linked syntactic opaqueness (here for the case-assignment rules) with the genericness of words, which we take to be semantic opaqueness.

3.6 Atomicity and the Mirror Principle

Baker (1985a) gives two sorts of arguments that the atomicity of words as outlined here is false and that syntax and morphology interpenetrate to a high degree. But we think a reasonable interpretation of the cases cited by Baker is consistent with the thesis of atomicity and, further, that the narrow range of interpenetrations witnessed by Baker and others is exactly the range expected under that thesis.

3.6.1 The Mirror Principle

Baker's first argument is that the fact that language observes what he calls the *Mirror Principle* indicates that syntactic rules are constituted of both syntactic and affixational operations, which of course is incompatible with the thesis of the syntactic atomicity of words. Though such an argument could be valid, the particular cases cited by Baker do not support it, because the syntactic operations he cites are arguably not syntactic but rather lexical; if this is so, then the Mirror Principle apparently amounts to nothing more than the compositionality of word formation.

The Mirror Principle says that affixes that correspond to syntactic operations, such as passive, causativization, agreement, and reflexivization, will be added onto the verb in the order in which these operations occur. As an illustration, consider the following case from Chamorro cited by Baker (p. 374):

(15) Hu#na'-fan-otchu   siha
     1sS-caus-pl-eat   them
     'I made them eat'

Here -*fan*-, a "plural subject" marker, is added before the causative; for this reason, according to the Mirror Principle, it registers the plurality of the precausativized "subject" of *eat* (*them*), even though *them* is not the surface subject. When -*fan*- appears on the outside of some affix, as it does in the case of the passive affix in this language, it registers a surface "subject's" plurality.

Baker argues from this that there are syntactic rules of causativization, plural number agreement, and passive and that, among other things, each rule adds an affix to the verb, thereby accounting for the morphological mirroring of the ordering of the syntactic operations.

We believe that this conclusion is not warranted and will outline why below. First, however, it is important to decide what one means by the term *syntactic*. If one means any rule that affects the syntactic distribution of a word or phrase, then no doubt all rules of morphology are "syntactic." This operational definition sheds little light on the articulation of grammatical theory into its subtheories. Based on his discussion of Chamorro, we conclude that Baker means something far more specific than this—by *syntactic rule* he means any rule whose domain of application is a syntactic phrase of some kind, that is, a rule that belongs to the phrase grammar of a language in the sense given earlier in this text. We approve of Baker's narrow sense of *syntactic*, for only such a narrow sense gives rise to interesting questions about the relation of syntax and morphology.

We think that Baker's examples fail to show that syntax and morphology are interrelated in the way he says, as long as syntax is understood narrowly. Here is why:

We suppose that any theory will have a lexicon, a list of the verbs and nouns of the language, each specified with various properties; verbs in particular will be specified as to the number, type, and deployment of their arguments, at a minimum; let us call this the *argument structure* of the verb. For example, *see* is specified as having a subject or "external" (underlined) argument and an internal Theme argument, as outlined in chapter 2:

(16) see (A̲, Th)

We assume further that on every view there will be rules of word formation not a part of the syntax, because their domain is simply the individual word, which derive words and their properties from other words or morphological material. Suppose that one thing a word formation rule can do is derive a word with an argument structure different from the argument structures of the word's parts. It is probably on this last supposition that Baker would depart from the view outlined. (See section 2.2.2 for further discussion and a specific proposal.) For example, an operation "externalizing" the Theme derives the adjectival past participle, as in (17):

(17) see (A̲, Th) → seen (A, T̲h̲)

This says that the Theme of the derived verb is the subject argument, and the Agent argument is internalized (see Williams 1979 and subsequent papers for discussion).

Note that such rules are not syntactic rules in the narrow sense, because the domain of application is not the phrase but rather (the argument structure of) the word.

We think it possible and advisable to construe Baker's rules as ones of this type, that is, as rules operating on the argument structure of verbs, and we will outline how. So construed, his rules are not syntactic in the narrow sense and do not refute the thesis of atomicity; further, the Mirror Principle becomes a special case of the thesis of the compositionality of word formation, a thesis surely required in any case.

Consider, for example, the interaction of causative, plural subject marking, and passive in Chamorro. Under the thesis adopted we must consider plural marking to be a lexical operation on the argument structure of verbs, and we must consider a verb's argument structures to potentially indicate restrictions on its arguments; we may then suppose the -*fan*- rule to be of the following kind:

(18) $\text{V } (\underline{X}, \ldots) \rightarrow \text{fan-V } (\underline{X}, \ldots)$
$$\begin{array}{c} | \\ \text{pl} \end{array}$$

The argument structure of *fan*-V has its external argument marked plural. Now suppose that causativization is another operation on argument structure, which adds a new (external) argument and internalizes the old external argument; further, it adds a prefix (*na'-* in Chamorro). If such a rule applies to a *fan*-V, the following structure will result:

(19) $\text{fan-V } (\underline{X}, \ldots) \rightarrow \text{na'-fan-V } (\underline{Y}, X, \ldots)$
$$\begin{array}{cc} | & | \\ \text{pl} & \text{pl} \end{array}$$

Both of these prefixes are added as a part of word formation, as operations on argument structures. The final form is a verb that can appear only with plural object arguments. This derivation does reflect a sort of mirror principle but only as a special case of the compositionality of word formation—the argument structure of the output of -*fan*- prefixation is the input argument structure for *na'-* prefixation.

The construal is possible even for the cases of anaphoric binding that Muysken (1981) gives and Baker repeats. As background to the discussion of these cases we will discuss a case of lexical anaphoric binding in English, the *self*- prefix. Whether prefix or noun stem, this item seems to result in the "anaphoric binding" of the Theme argument by the Actor argument. For example, we have the following:

(20) educated (A, Th) → self-educated (A_i, Th_i)
     denial $(\underline{R}, A, Th)$ → self-denial $(\underline{R}, A_i, Th_i)$

The A_i notation indicates the binding of the first argument by the second.

We take this to establish that there is this kind of argument binding as an operation on argument structures of lexical items. One could of course try to make this a case of syntactic binding, insisting that *self-* was bound by a syntactic rule to the syntactic subject and that the *self-* was syntactically related to the object position of *educated*:

(21) a. John$_i$ was self$_i$-educated
     b. [PRO$_i$ self$_i$-denial] is fun

In the case of *self-denial* one must claim that there is a PRO NP "subject" of the NP to serve as antecedent. This becomes doubtful, however, for cases in which *self-denial* is not itself the head of the word in which it appears:

(22) [Self-denial reactions]$_N$ should be checked

Assuming that *self-denial* is simply the first member of an N–N compound, there is no syntactic subject available to serve as antecedent; yet the word seems to have the same meaning in (22) as in (21b).

A further and more important reason for not syntactifying the interpretation of *self-* has to do with the strict limitation on its binder—it must be a coargument, a restriction that does not hold of its (truly) syntactic cousin *himself.* But this restriction is exactly what one expects if the binding is purely morphological—only the argument structure of the form to which *self-* is attached can be affected.

Given that there is such binding of arguments by arguments in the argument structure of verbs, we might wonder what relation this has to syntactic binding, how much it overlaps with it, and so on, and whether we might get rid of one in favor of the other, if there is great redundancy of mechanisms. We will return to this important question in the next section. For the time being we will simply assume that there are such operations on argument structure as the reflexive binding just illustrated.

We may now consider the Quechua cases reported by Muysken. Quechua has a reciprocal suffix, *-naku*, which we may associate with the binding of arguments just discussed: the Theme is bound by the Actor of verbs to which this affix is attached. Quechua also has a causativizing affix, with which we may associate the same operation on argument structure that we posited for the Chamorro causative: add a new external argument and internalize the old external argument. Given this and the interesting fact that the causative suffix may be added either before or after the reciprocal suffix, we predict two outcomes—the causativized reciprocal and the reciprocalized causative:

(23) a. verb-recip-caus

      (new-A, old-A$_i$, Th$_i$)

   b. verb-caus-recip

      (new-A$_i$, old-A, Th$_i$)

Both cases exist, with predictably different meanings (see Muysken 1981 and the discussion in Baker 1985a, (39)–(40)).

Clearly the existence of these cases under the construal given does not demonstrate any kind of interpenetration of syntax and morphology—the operations in each case are on the argument structure of individual words. If binding of arguments by arguments in argument structures is available at all, then these examples are not to the point.

An argument of Baker's that would seem to resist defusing in the above manner concerns the interaction of causativization and reflexive binding in Chi-Mwi:ni. Chi-Mwi:ni has a causative suffix just like the ones discussed: it inserts a new external argument and internalizes the old external argument (it becomes the accusative object, and the old accusative object becomes oblique). Chi-Mwi:ni also has a "free" reflexive (like English) rather than a reflexive affix. This reflexive can appear only in direct object position. The one exception to this is in a causative construction, where it can appear in the oblique direct object position. This kind of exception can be explained, so the argument runs, only if the reflexive is in its syntactic position as an accusative direct object at the point where the causative affix is added, but this is possible if affixation and syntactic rules are intermingled in the way that the atomicity thesis denies.

In a grammar wthout intermingling the syntactic rule of reflexive binding apparently would need to be sensitive to the prior morphological derivation of the verb in order to know exactly which oblique objects are exempt from the restriction of the reflexive pronoun to the accusative object position.

But suppose that the reflexive binding is not syntactic but lexical, as in the other cases that we have discussed. We might suppose that the reflexive rule is an operation on argument structures that adds no affix but rather adds the feature "refl" to the specification of the accusative argument of verbs and binds the Theme argument to the subject argument. The "refl" feature on the accusative argument means that only the reflexive pronoun can be inserted in the position associated with this argument in syntax.

This scheme will give us the correct distribution of the reflexive pronoun, in particular its occurrence in oblique object position in causatives, as long as we permit the causative rule to apply after the reflexive rule and not before:

(24) V ($\underline{A}$, Th, ...) → V ($\underline{new\text{-}A}$, old-A, Th)
      acc   acc   obl
      refl   refl

This solution has an ad hoc air about it because it seems to code the distribution of reflexives in the lexical representations of verbs. We will return to this ad-hocness in section 3.6.2. It is important to distinguish this ad-hocness from another—namely, that of restricting causativization to precede the marking of verbs as taking reflexive accusative arguments. This last ad-hocness is common to both theories in that the ordering of rules must be stipulated; so neither theory actually predicts that nonaccusative reflexives will be found. Baker bases his argument on something weaker than prediction, namely, that the interpenetration of syntax and morphology permits a description, whereas the strong lexicalist hypothesis does not. We have seen that the latter supposition is not so, strictly speaking, uneasy though we may be about the feature "refl."

3.6.2 How Lexical Rules Differ from Syntactic Rules

The "refl" feature used to counter Baker's claim that at least some affixation must be done in syntax might seem at first glance simply to insulate the atomicity thesis against all possible empirical challenge. This is not so. Even with the use of such features, the thesis has great empirical content, content with no analogue in theories that deny it.

That great empirical content is this: the atomicity thesis says that morphological rules can operate only on what is represented in the argument structure of verbs. This is part of the general inescapable feature of morphological rules: that they operate only on lexical information (and not on syntactic configurations). Thus an affix added to a verb can alter only *that verb*'s argument structure; further, any alteration of a verb's argument structure must be associated with an affix added *to that verb* and not to some other word in the sentence in which that verb might appear.

Let us now return to the ad-hocness of the "refl" feature in Chi-Mwi:ni. In light of the remarks just made, the feature is less ad hoc than it might appear. First, any theory must account for the fact that the reflexive pronoun can only appear in the accusative object position; there is no reason a priori that this restriction should be syntactic rather than morphological. A morphological treatment is possible only because the reflexive in Chi-Mwi:ni is confined to a particular argument position. The English reflexive cannot be morphologically bound, for example, for the reflexive and antecedent are not always arguments of the same lexical item:

(25) John saw pictures of himself

Thus making the Chi-Mwi:ni reflexive a morphologically bound reflexive automatically restricts the reflexivization to argument structure mates. Further, the morphological theory predicts that only morphological reflexives can interact with causativization as the Chi-Mwi:ni reflexive does— so the English reflexive could show no such interaction if it were imported into Chi-Mwi:ni.

Suppose that we use the phrase *strongly morphological* to refer to a rule that *could be* stated as an operation on argument structures and the phrase *strongly syntactic* for a rule that could not be. The terminology is meant to be theory-neutral because it does not presume what the correct analysis of the strongly morphological cases will be. From the above discussion, we conclude that the Chi-Mwi:ni reflexive and causative are strongly morphological, whereas the English reflexive is strongly syntactic. The lexicalist hypothesis then makes the prediction that strongly morphological rules cannot be "fed" by strongly syntactic rules. No such prediction is made by the theory that Baker outlines. From this point of view, the "refl" feature is not so ad hoc after all because it embodies this strong restriction on the kind of reflexive that the language can have and, further, on the kind of reflexive that could possibly interact with affixal causativization. It seems to us that the theory Baker outlines, which allows free interspersal of morphological and syntactic operations, makes no such predictions.

The question can legitimately be raised, How does the Chi-Mwi:ni child learn that its language has a morphological reflexive, since it is not affixal? Perhaps this is the first guess that the child makes, as "Theme bound by Actor" seems to be the central case of reflexivization, and perhaps only in the face of positive evidence that the relation is strongly syntactic, as would be found in English, does the child abandon the morphological binding.

This discussion provokes a more general question: What is the relation between the position of an affix in a sentence and the effect of that affix on the logical organization of the sentence? We think that the lexicalist hypothesis makes quite a strong answer: an affix can affect the argument structure of only the item to which it is attached. The kinds of rules that Baker discusses, which contain both syntactic and affixational operations, do not seem to make this prediction. Why is there no rule that adds an affix to one verb but causativizes some other? Or adds an affix to the noun subject and binds a reflexive object? Such rules can be written in the notation that Baker informally presents; they could be shown to be consistent with the Mirror Principle; and they could not easily be distinguished from the kinds of rules that Baker does propose. We might canonize this observation that no such rules exist as a "relevance" principle: affixes can only be added to the word whose argument structure is relevant to the syntactic operation of the rule. But this principle is a natural consequence of the separation of affixation and syntax under the atomicity thesis, just as the Mirror Principle is a natural consequence of the compositionality of word formation.

A similar dilemma arises when one considers the scope of the syntactic rules in a theory that does not observe the atomicity of words. In Baker's theory rules that alter the "grammatical functions" are syntactic rules (in the narrow sense described earlier)—causativization, for example, turns subject into object. These rules also alter the argument structure of lexical items; causativization, for example, turns a verb with x arguments into one with $x + 1$ arguments. Given this, one must ask, What is the scope of syntactic rules? For example, are nominalizations derived in syntax? A nominalizer such as -*ion* alters the argument structure of verbs to which it is added in that it internalizes the external argument of the verb it attaches to and adds an external argument (in this regard, it is identical to causativization). One cannot appeal here to a distinction between "derivational" and "inflectional" affixes without utterly begging the question.

In a theory in which affixation is entirely removed from syntax, the answer is simple: though there may be rules that alter grammatical functions (namely, NP-Movement), there are no syntactic rules that alter argument structure. So the question of the scope of syntactic rules is firmly fixed: nominalization, for example, cannot be a syntactic operation; it is strictly a morphological operation.

3.6.3 Noun Incorporation

Baker (1983, 1985) presents another kind of challenge to the atomicity thesis, in that he develops a view of noun-incorporating languages that is inconsistent with it.

The phenomenon of noun incorporation is illustrated in the following sentences from Iroquoian (Baker 1983, 6):

(26) a. I?i ye-k-hreks ne   yeokar
       I   tl-1s-push prefix prefix-bark
       'I push the bark'
    b. I?i ye-k-kar-hreks-s
       I   tl-1s-bark-push
       'I bark push'

Here the direct object of *push* in (26a) has been incorporated into the verb in (26b). A syntactic theory might derive (26b) from (26a) by movement in syntax. Such a view of noun incorporation is offered by Baker (1983, 1985).

However, perhaps the incorporated noun is added to the verb as an act of word formation, governed by the principles of morphology. Such an analysis, call it the *compounding* or *morphological* analysis, posits no syntactic relation between (26a) and (26b). Among the possibilities of compounding consistent with the principles laid out above and in chapter 2 is that the first element of the incorporated structure might affect the argument structure of the second element:

(27) kar + hreks → kar-hreks
      (A̱, Th) (A̱, Th)
              |
            kar

The change in the argument structure is the following: *kar* is added as a qualifier on the Theme argument of *hreks*. It does not satisfy the argument structure (though in Mithun's (1983) type I–III languages this is what happens); rather it sets conditions on the reference of the θ-role (in our view θ-roles themselves refer, not the overt NPs to which they are linked). Given the availability of these two analyses, the morphological and the syntactic, how does one choose?

Baker (1983, 1985) has given four arguments that noun incorporation is syntactic, not morphological or compounding. The arguments are as follows:

1. When a noun incorporates, remnants of its syntactic NP position may remain behind (Baker 1983, 13; from Postal 1962, 285):

ka-nuhs-raku   thiku
3n-house-white this

2. A copy may be left behind:

ka-nuhs-raku   thiku ka-nuhs-a
3n-house-white this   pre-house-suf

3. Only objects and subjects of intransitives can be incorporated (this characterization is "syntactic").

4. Incorporated nouns may introduce discourse referents; thus they are syntactically or referentially transparent.

Before turning to a critique of these arguments, let us consider what kind of analysis of incorporation is permitted by the thesis of syntactic atomicity. It does not permit a movement rule of the kind proposed by Baker.

It requires that the compounding of verb and noun be done without reference to its syntactic environment and, further, that the relation of a verb (and its argument structure) to its arguments be done without reference to the internal structure of the verb. These strictures on the possible analyses of noun-incorporated structures make predictions quite different from those made by Baker's analysis.

The compounding or "qualifier" theory of noun incorporation outlined above is strictly within the narrow bounds allowed by the atomicity thesis. Recall from chapter 2 that a morphological operation can affect the syntactic distribution of the resulting word in only two ways: it can affect the features on that word or it can affect the argument structure of that word. Thus the atomicity thesis creates a "bottleneck" in the passage of information from morphemes to the syntactic environment. The qualifier theory falls under the second of these possibilities because the incorporated noun becomes a qualifier on one of the arguments of the verb. In syntax a verb with such a qualification will have a different distribution from a verb without such a qualification, but under the atomicity thesis that distribution must be a function strictly of the qualification itself and not of how the qualification came to be there. It might appear that the ability to affect both the features and argument structure of a lexical item fairly much evacuates the atomicity thesis, but we again emphasize that without the atomicity thesis many other things are possible; for example, an incorporated noun conceivably could affect the argument structure of a verb other than the one into which the noun is incorporated (see section 4.3 for a discussion of this point).

The atomicity thesis further predicts that the syntax of syntactic arguments will be independent of whether or not there is an incorporated noun on the verb.

With these general remarks about the morphological theory in mind, we will now consider in turn Baker's four arguments for the syntactic analysis of noun incorporation.

First, the possibility of leaving an NP remnant behind is independent of incorporation and thus cannot count as an argument of it (Mohawk; Mithun 1983, (106)–(107)):

(28) a. Kanekwarunyu wa'-k-akyatawi'tsher-u:ni
       it.dotted.DIST PAST-I-dress-mark
       'I dress-made a polka-dotted one'
   b. Kanekwarunyu wa'katkahtho
       it.dotted.DIST PAST.I.see
       'I saw a polka-dotted one'

In (28a) it looks like incorporation has left behind a remnant of the NP it has been extracted from; however, (28b) shows that the existence of such remnant NPs is independent of incorporation. The independence of remnant NPs from the process of incorporation is exactly what one expects under the compounding theory. Though compatible, it is not expected under the movement theory; it is accidental.

Baker considers the existence of "copies" of the incorporated noun to be a argument for syntactic movement, by analogy with clitic doubling structures (and the assumption that they are syntactic). However, copies not only exist, inexact copies exist (Mohawk; Mithun 1983, (105)):

(29) ... sha'te:ku niku:ti rabahbot wahu-tsy-ahni:nu ki...

      eight   of.them bullhead he-fish-bought

   '[he] bought eight bullheads'

It strains our formal sensibilities to call *fish* a copy of *bullhead*. Rather it appears that what is inside and what is outside the V are more or less independent of each other (except that the Novelty Constraint of Wasow 1972 might apply), and the exact copy is just a special case. These strongly support the predicted independence of the expression of syntactic arguments from the process of incorporation, as predicted by the atomicity thesis.

The question of what can be incorporated deserves comment. Baker claims that only objects of transitives and subjects of certain intransitives can incorporate. If one assumes that these intransitives are "ergative" in that their S-Structure subject is a D-Structure object, then incorporation targets a D-Structure natural class: direct objects. This "syntactic" characterization implies that the rule is syntactic, not lexical.

Granting the generalization, it is far from clear that the rule is syntactic. After all, direct objects are arguments of the verb, and there is no reason to think that the targets of noun incorporation could not be the specification of these arguments in the argument structure of verbs. A convincing demonstration of the syntactic nature of the rule would be a "direct object" that was not an argument of the verb, as are found in the English raising passives. No such case is given. The closest is the possessor raising cases, for which the point is moot (consider English *I hit Bill's head, I hit Bill in the head*).

Baker (1985) explicitly argues against a characterization of the target of noun incorporation as being the θ-role Theme. First he gives Gruber's (1965) definition of Theme:

(30) The *theme* of a given predicate is the argument which
     moves or is located in that predication.

Then he cites the following example as one in ·which the target of noun
incorporation cannot be Theme, because fields do not move when one
reaches them (Baker 1985, (45); quoting Hewitt 1903):

(31) Hakare' nen' ia'-e'-hent-ara'ne' ka-'hent-owane'
     after   now tl-3F-field-reached pre-field-large
     'Then after awhile she reached a grassy clearing that was large'

However, it is not at all clear that the notion "Theme" is to be so narrowly
understood; for example, if we follow the conventional analysis, *field* must
be Theme in (32):

(32) The field is reachable

Further, Baker (1985, 57) himself gives a principle relating thematic
structure to syntactic structure that would seem to undermine his argument
in any case:

(33) Identical thematic relationships between items are
     represented by identical structural relationships
     between those items at the level of D-structure.

Given that *field* in (31) is incorporated and thus must be a D-Structure
object in Baker's theory, and given that it is not a Theme, then (33) implies
that some other θ role, such as Goal, can be realized in object position and
therefore cannot be realized in any other way, a highly unlikely conclusion.

In any case we see no need to construe "Theme" in the narrow way that
Baker does and in fact believe that the cognitive content of "Theme" is
very slight. This is not to say that there will be no empirical difference
between Baker's proposal and ours—for example, our proposal (but not
his) implies that the incorporated noun must be an argument of the
incorporating verb.

Finally, incorporation in general is not limited to direct objects or
Themes. Baker himself is forced to adopt a preposition insertion rule (for
Nieuan) to preserve his generalization that direct objects alone incorporate; Mithun (1983, 875f.) discusses a number of languages in which
instruments and locations incorporate.

Baker's last argument is that the ability of incorporated nouns to introduce discourse referents argues for the syntactic nature of noun incorporation, the assumption being that only syntactic positions, not parts of words,
can perform this function. The argument itself has one troubling feature:
clearly Baker is adopting some idea of the opacity of words in making this

argument, because he is assuming that parts of words are referentially opaque; however, it is not clear why this opacity does not prohibit noun incorporation itself.

In any case Mithun (1983, 871) explicitly addresses this argument: "It is the pronominal system . . . that differs from English, not the word formation process." And she gives the following example to illustrate (Mohawk; Mithun 1983, (112)):

(34) K-atenun-hah-kwe. Ah tis   yehetkv
     I-watch-HAB-PAST ah how she.ugly
     'I was baby-sitting. Boy, is she ugly'

In this example *watch*, which does not have a noun incorporated, nevertheless serves to introduce a referent, which the subsequent pronoun *she* picks up. Naturally, introduction of discourse referents is also possible with noun incorporation; this example simply shows that it is independent of that process.

In sum it appears that all the phenomena Baker cites as evidence of the syntactic nature of noun incorporation are independent of the process itself—the ability to have remnants of NPs without heads, to have null NPs, and to introduce discourse referents. This independence is exactly what one would expect under the morphological analysis of noun incorporation, because the kind of dependence imputed in each case would be impossible due to the "bottleneck" imposed by the hypothesis of the syntactic opacity of morphological objects. This bottleneck gives rise to a far more specific set of expectations that seem thoroughly accurate.

Baker (1985) develops an incorporation account for a good many constructions beyond the case of noun incorporation; for example, preposition incorporation (for constructions like the English dative constructions) and verb incorporation (for the causative constructions). We will not attempt to treat all these here, confining ourselves to the following few remarks. In his extremely wide-ranging and informative discussion of these constructions, he repeatedly asserts that the incorporated item is the head of the category that is the complement of the incorporating verb (just as in the case of noun incorporation). It is important to realize that this observation, which we take to be "correct" (though of course not literally true), does not favor the view of syntactic incorporation over the one outlined here. This is exactly what we would expect. The compounding we posit for noun-incorporating languages results in an alteration in argument structure. The θ-roles of an argument structure are assigned under (very tight) government. Therefore, even under the pure compounding view of incorporation, we expect that the compounding will directly affect the governed arguments, and nothing else.

3.7 Inflection

It is common in the field of grammar to draw a distinction between inflectional and derivational affixes, and it is common in generative grammar to assign derivational affixes to the lexicon proper and inflectional affixes to syntax. A number of accounts, however, do not draw this distinction in this way, assigning all affixation to the rules of morphology; among them are the accounts of Williams (1978) and Lapointe (1979).

Our view of morphology as strictly the science of word form compels us to ask, Are derivational and inflectional affixes formally different? It appears that they are not—any devices available for one kind of process also seem to be available for the other. The separation of affixes into derivational and inflectional ones seems entirely a matter of interpretation, not of form. It is roughly true that some affixes have more syntactic consequences than others, but it would be best to explain this in terms of the intrinsic properties of the affixes themselves rather than by simply assigning each affix to one of the two groups.

The work of Anderson (1982) is a recent defense of the derivation versus inflection distinction and of the view that the distinction corresponds to how syntax is organized. He defines *inflectional morphology* as follows (p. 587):

(35) Inflectional morphology is what is relevant to the syntax.

We believe that this definition fails to divide up affixes in the way that Anderson intends and that essentially the fault is not correctible because the distinction is a phantom to begin with. This definition would seem to consign all nominalizing affixes, like *-ion*, to inflection because nouns and verbs have different syntactic properties, and the affix makes the difference. So the suffix *-ion* permits the verb *construct* in (36) to appear in the subject position:

(36) The construction was nice

This is perfectly parallel to the fact that the suffix *-s* permits the singular noun *horse* in (37) to appear as the subject of a plural VP:

(37) The horses were nice

Anderson's definition does not separate these two cases.

Affixes that affected the argument structure of verbs would also count as inflectional in Anderson's theory. So the prefix *out-*, which transitivizes verbs, would be inflectional because it affects the syntactic environment of the verb to which it attaches. These cases are surely not intended to count as inflectional. The problem is not with the definition but with the distinction itself, which cannot be defended in any form that would correspond to our ordinary intuitions.

Then where do our ordinary intuitions about the distinction come from? They derive plainly from the fact that some affixes have more syntactic relevance than others. But we may account for this in terms of the affixes themselves. For example, *-s* bears the syntactically relevant feature of plurality; *re-*, however, bears no syntactically relevant features. We believe that nothing further need be said to account for the difference in behavior of these two affixes; in particular it is not necessary to assign them to different subcomponents of morphology, or one to syntax and the other to morphology.

Anderson bases an argument for the assignment of inflectional affixes to syntax on the observation that inflectional affixes occur outside derivational affixes. Because we do not accept the distinction, we would rephrase the observation as follows: affixes more relevant to syntax appear outside affixes less relevant to syntax. This observation was explained by Williams (1978, 1981) and in chapter 2 in terms of the given definition of head and the feature percolation mechanism implied by that definition. Briefly, syntactically relevant affixes appear on the periphery of words because only there can their features determine the features of the word as a whole, and only when the features of the affix determine the features of the whole can it affect the syntactic properties of the whole. With this account of the observation available, it is not necessary to bifurcate the theory of morphology in the way that Anderson proposes.

Anderson bases another argument for the distinction, and for the syntactic status of inflectional affixes, on some observations concerning Breton verb agreement: in Breton a verb agrees with a subject only if the subject is null. Anderson accounts for this by positing that a pronoun can be generated in subject position and cliticized onto the verb, where later rules of morphology will convert the clitic-verb combination into a verb with an inflectional affix. When the subject is filled with a lexical NP, there will be no cliticization and consequently no inflectional affix. The analysis depends, then, on a certain interpenetration of syntax and morphology: the morphological rules of inflection must follow the sentence-level rule of cliticization.

There is an alternative account that observes the atomicity thesis. Suppose that the agreement marker had the property of "satisfying" the θ-role assigned to the subject. The agreement marker is then similar to other affixes, such as the transitivizing affix *out-* in English (*outrun*), that alter the argument structure of verbs. From this it follows that if the verb bears the agreement marker, the subject must be null, for the subject position will not be assigned a θ-role, and any subject would therefore violate the θ-Criterion. However, if the subject were empty and the verb did not bear the agreement marker, this too would violate the θ-Criterion, for the subject θ-role would not be satisfied.

English actually has a morphological process formally similar to the agreement marker in Breton in that it involves word-internal argument satisfaction. This is compounding:

(38) *John is a book-reader of books

This example is odd because the object θ-role of *read* is satisfied inside the compound *book-reader*, so the argument *books* violates the θ-Criterion.

Given that word-internal θ-role satisfaction must be available as a general device, it is not necessary to posit the interpenetration of syntax and morphology that Anderson proposes to account for his observations about Breton agreement.

Anderson in fact proposes a variant of his view that does not rely on cliticization. If the inflectional affix were a pronoun subject to Principle B of the binding theory, he reasons, it could not cooccur with a subject it was coindexed with because that would result in a violation of Principle B. But like the first solution, this one violates the atomicity of words in that the affix must be "visible" to Principle B despite the fact that the affix is inside a word; so we reject this account as well.

Both of Anderson's accounts fail to say why it is not possible to omit both the agreement and the subject NP in Breton, so something further must be said. If the θ-Criterion is invoked to explain this fact, as it is in our alternative to Anderson's account, it will render redundant his cliticization mechanism for the explanation of the other facts.

We are then left with no reason to distinguish inflectional and derivational affixes, and in fact much reason not to distinguish them: their formal similarity.

3.8 Bracketing Paradoxes

Williams (1978, 1981) proposed that certain paradoxes in morphology could be resolved by regarding "relatedness" among lexical items to be a phenomenon not fully reflecting the morphological structure of lexical items.

For example, the word *hydroelectricity* has the following structure:

(39)

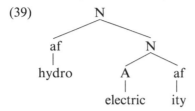

But this word is clearly related to *hydroelectric*, from which it cannot be derived by affixation because *-ity* is a class I affix (in the terminology of Allen 1978 and Selkirk 1982) and cannot be added to a word beginning with a class II affix like *hydro*. So this "relatedness" cannot be expressed by morphological structure.

Williams (1981) proposed that "relatedness" of lexical items could be obtained by creating "constellations" of related words according to the following definition:

(40) X is related to Y if X can be gotten from Y by substituting for a head of Y, including substituting 0 for a head of Y.

So *hydroelectric* can be derived from *hydroelectricity* by substituting 0 for the head *-ity* of Y.

Clearly this redefinition of "relatedness" will relate words that are not morphologically derivable from one another. It defines a semantic relation that is not compositional. At the same time, though, it does not permit every possible kind of relation, because the substituting is restricted to heads.

Pesetsky (1985) has proposed another solution to the bracketing paradoxes. He proposes that they be solved by importing the Quantifier Rule (QR) from syntax into morphology, and so this rule is not compatible with the atomicity thesis.

The atomicity thesis compels us to resist Pesetsky's suggestion. This is not so much because adding QR to morphology would make it too "syntactic"—after all, we already have phrase structure and the notion "head" in both syntax and morphology—but rather because the bracketing paradoxes span syntax and morphology. For example, the syntactic phrases *transformational grammar* and *transformational grammarian* are "related" exactly as *hydroelectricity* and *hydroelectric* are:

(41) a.

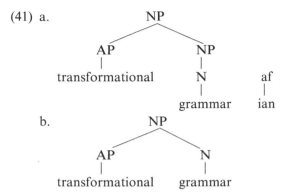

b.

An important feature of the redefinition of "relatedness" given above is that it was purely "interpretive"—that is, it was not part of the rules of formation of either syntax or morphology. QR, however, is a rule of formation, and the representation it derives, LF, is part of the structural description of the objects to which it applies. Some of the bracketing paradoxes, such as (41), span syntax and morphology; therefore any solution to bracketing paradoxes runs the risk of violating the atomicity thesis.[4]

Pesetsky proposes to solve the paradoxes by having QR move the affix that is in the wrong position:

(42)   [hydro [electric ity]]   → [[hydroelectric t] ity]
        morphological structure   LF

The *t* in the output is the trace of the moved affix. The LF representation in (42) accurately expresses the meaning of the form in that it says that the form is a nominalization of *hydroelectric*.

Though Pesetsky does not discuss examples like (41), his reasoning applied here leads to the same conclusion: QR applies:

(43) [[transformational]   [grammar ian]]$_{NP}$ →
     [[[transformational] [grammar t]]$_{NP}$ ian]$_{NP}$

This derivation violates the atomicity thesis because a rule applying in a syntactic domain has removed part of a word. Because Pesetsky's QR solution implicates such derivations, it is in conflict with the atomicity thesis. In this section we will examine Pesetsky's arguments that QR can apply so as to move morphemes, and we will conclude that they are unwarranted.

4. There may in fact be no structural solution to the problem posed by this example. Quite parallel to (41) is "renal surgeon," but there is no related verb "renal surge."

Pesetsky first bases an argument on the observation that certain prefixations are incompatible with idiomatic interpretations; for example, *unrarity* is not the negation of *rarity* in the sense in which it occurs in *That book is a real rarity*. He attributes this to the fact that the LF structure of *unrarity* will be as follows,

(44) [[unrar t] ity]

and that the rule that assigns *rarity* its idiomatic interpretation cannot apply here because *rarity* is not a constituent in LF. This argument ignores the fact that many movements leave idiomatic interpretations unchanged; for example, Wh-Movement:

(45) What kind of tabs do you keep t on Bill

In the theory solving the paradoxes by redefining "relatedness," it is no surprise that *unrarity* cannot be related to *rarity* in its idiomatic interpretation. In receiving a special interpretation *rarity* forgoes a position in a constellation, so *unrarity* cannot be related to it by a constellation-defining operation; *unrarity* can be related only to *unrare*. Important here is Pesetsky's observation that the words are idiomatic—that is, their meaning is not derived by regular rule. Our account depends on this. Pesetsky's account, on the other hand, actually depends on there being a rule assigning the idiomatic interpretation. This seems to us a nearly paradoxical use of the term *rule*.

A fully general rule of QR in morphology would move affixes in a wide variety of cases in which its utility, or even its benignity, is in question. Pesetsky, incorrectly in our opinion, argues that some of the peculiar cases of this type do exist. For example, suppose QR in morphology moves one affix over another. Then a word with two affixes will be ambiguous (just as a sentence with two quantifiers is ambiguous). Pesetsky claims that each of the following is ambiguous:

(46) a. mis-re-match
      b. re-mis-match

We simply dispute this judgment. And the same for the following pair from Spanish:

(47) a. esfer   oid ita
          sphere like diminutive
      b. esfer   it   oid
          sphere diminutive like

Again, we simply dispute the judgments. It is quite easy to understand how the meanings of the (a) and (b) pairs in (46) and (47) could become confused, but this does not mean that they are synonymous.

Hedging this prediction, Pesetsky discusses the possiblity that the applications of QR in morphology are string-vacuous; that is, they cannot effect the reordering of morphemes and so cannot introduce the ambiguities claimed for (46) and (47). We think that this is certainly a move in the right direction, though it undercuts the idea that movement is involved if string-vacuousness is enforced.

It seems that a further restriction is required to rule out the following derivation:

(48) imperfection conscious →
    [im [perfection conscious]]

Such a derivation would imply that *imperfection conscious* could mean 'unconscious of perfections', which it does not. This kind of derivation could be eliminated by restricting QR to heads, because the derivation in (48) involves the movement of a nonhead.

But if QR is restricted to applying string-vacuously and to moving heads, then it is identical in empirical import to the redefinition of "relatedness" proposed by Williams (1978, 1981).

So restricted, the rule looks very little like syntactic QR. In fact additional features make it appear even less like QR in syntax. Pesetsky's final argument is one for the trace of QR in morphology. He observes that compounding that saturates the external argument of the head of the compound is ungrammatical (as noted in Williams 1981, 1984, and Selkirk 1982). He cites the following kind of example to illustrate this:

(49) *weather changing

His argument assumes that *weather* is the external argument of *changing* and that the structure after QR is as follows:

(50) [weather [[change t]] ing]

Here the movement rule has moved the affix out of a category containing a "subject"—so, Pesetsky reasons, (49) is ungrammatical because of the Specified Subject Condition.

The argument is based on an empirical mistake. Actually *the weather* is an internal argument in (49), as (51) shows:

(51) the changing of the weather

The same applies to Pesetsky's other examples.

Pesetsky's argument also has conceptual flaws. First, it assumes that QR is obligatory, which is inconsistent with assumptions about QR in syntax.

Second, QR in syntax is not subject to the Specified Subject Condition, so it is unclear why QR in morphology should be. Finally, as explained by Williams (1981, 1984), the saturation of the external argument in compounding is impossible in general, in a wider range of cases than those in which QR can be invoked; for example, the following:

(52) It was house-white (meaning 'The house is white')

In sum it appears that there is no reason to import QR into morphology. The restrictions that must be placed on it in morphology make it empirically equivalent to the "head-relatedness" theory of Williams (1981) anyway, and the atomicity thesis is severely compromised in light of examples like (41).

3.9   Conclusion

In chapter 2 we outlined the rules of word formation, and in this chapter we have argued that the objects defined by these rules are opaque to syntactic rules: the lexicalist hypothesis.

The percolation of features through heads and the reference to the argument structures of lexical items, both of which occur in syntax and morphology, allow for a great deal of indirect interaction between affixes and the syntactic environment, exactly what is attested, it appears, and perhaps no more. The "word" is in a sense a "bottleneck" in the passage of information from the morphological to the syntactic, and the purpose of this chapter has been to demonstrate that this bottleneck is exactly wide enough.

We might consider the system outlined in chapter 2 to be the "core" of morphology, and this core relates to syntax in the way just mentioned.

However, we have already discussed two phenomena that extend beyond this "core"—the "reanalysis" discussed in section 3.3 and the "relatedness" phenomena discussed in section 3.8. In both cases syntax and morphology are intermingled in a way that goes beyond the shared vocabulary of features and argument structures—in reanalysis a syntactic string is made a "word" by fiat, and the definition of "relatedness" spans syntax and morphology. In chapter 4 we will take up further phenomena of this type.

Our assignment of these processes to the periphery commits us to the usual ideas about peripheral phenomena—that they will be learned late, that they will be subject to variation and instability over time, tending to revert to the general lines of the core, and so on.

However, at present our best evidence for the special status of these phenomena is that they do not fit in the core and can be best understood as specific kinds of deviation from the core. Specifically, we will posit in chapter 4 that certain structures that deviate from the core are characterized by the fact that two analyses, rather than a single analysis, must hold of them, where each analysis by itself is well formed according to the core, and that the special properties of these constructions flow from this dual analysis.

Chapter 4

Nonmorphological Objects

So far we have considered "pure" morphology and have argued that it is distinct from syntax in two ways. First, it is a generative system (like syntax) that simply generates a different set of objects than the set that syntax generates. Second, we have argued that the principles of formation and the vocabulary of the systems of syntax and morphology are distinct (though they overlap).

The division of the world into "syntactic objects" and "morphological objects" leaves little room for the interpenetration of syntax and morphology, which we believe to be correct; in general the interpenetration is limited to what information can be passed through the narrow window of shared vocabulary. Syntax determines the distribution in sentences of such objects as "plural Ns"; morphology determines the form of such objects as "plural Ns," and this is as far as the interpenetration goes. Syntax cannot tell, for example, how a plural N came to be one from the morphological point of view or how a word came to have any of the properties that it has. At least, this is the point of view that we adopt here.

In this chapter we will consider cases in which the line that separates syntax and morphology seems to blur. We will examine words (in the sense of "syntactic atom") that have the internal structure of syntactic phrases, and we will examine the notion of "word" that is required in the analysis of reanalyzed, or "coanalyzed," structures. In both cases we consider it possible to isolate the interpenetration of syntax and morphology in such a way that the generality of the laws in the two systems is not compromised.

4.1 Syntactic Words

Let us call anything that can be inserted into an X^0 position in syntax a *syntactic atom*. "Syntactic atom" and "morphological object" are not coextensive concepts, and we will discuss the difference in this section.

Syntactic atomicity holds for a class of objects that do not have a morphological form but otherwise display the general properties of X^0s. The form of these objects is phrasal even though they are inserted in X^0 positions. We will refer to them by the expression *syntactic words*. Given that the properties of their form do not follow from the morphological laws, we will consider them to be marked objects. The rules creating these objects essentially reanalyze a phrase as a word. These rules are part of the grammar of word formation of French, German, English, Italian, and in fact probably all languages.

Essentially we will argue that what have been called compounds in French and Italian are not compounds at all in the sense in which English has compounds but are rather "reanalyzed" phrases.

4.1.1 Syntactic Words Versus Syntactic Objects

Syntactic words must first be distinguished from listed syntactic phrases of the kind discussed in chapter 1, such as French *en voir de toutes les couleurs* 'to have a hard time'. These are phrasal idioms, that is, phrases that happen to be listed because of their noncompositional meaning. They are not syntactically atomic—for example, the case just cited allow the clitic *en* to be extracted, as discussed in chapter 1.

The syntactic words that are the subject of this section are all syntactically atomic. For this reason we will say that the syntactic words are instances of X^0, and that the listed phrases are instances not of X^0 but of X^{max}.

The so-called Romance compounds are a candidate set of syntactic words, as discussed by Di Sciullo (1981a). These words contain a verb and a complement of some kind:

(1) a. V + N: essui-glace, attrape-nigaud, rabat-joie
b. V + A: gagne-petit, sent-bon, pense-bête
c. V + Adv: couche-tard, lève-tôt, passe-partout
d. V + P: frappe-devant, saute-dessus

These forms are instances of X^0, insertable in syntax into N positions (*l'essui-glace* 'the windshield wiper'; *un bon essui-glace* 'a good windshield wiper'), and thus they differ from the forms discussed in section 1.2 (idioms, or listed syntactic units) such as *take NP to task* and *voir en de toutes les couleurs*, which are listed VPs, insertable only into X^{max} positions. These two cases also differ with respect to syntactic atomicity, as we have just remarked. Syntactic atomicity holds for syntactic words but not for the listed syntactic phrases that we call phrasal idioms. We have seen that clitic placement applies to *en voir de toutes les couleurs* so as to remove the clitic from it and that the reference assignment rule applies to the NP in *take NP to task* in the normal way. Hence these items do not exhibit the opacity to syntactic rule that we expect of words.

By contrast, syntactic words like those in (1) are instances of X^0 and thus syntactic atoms. No syntactic rule can insert or move a category in the structure, as shown in (2). In (2a) the Adv *bien* 'well' has been inserted in the word, in (2b) and (2c) Move α has applied. Their ungrammaticality follows from syntactic atomicity if they are X^0s, which are the atoms of syntax:

(2) a. *essui-bien glace
        wipe well windshield
    b. *[glace essui e]
    c. *Glace   a   été réparé   cet [essui e] par Jean
        windshield has been repaired this wipe   by Jean

Further, no reference assignment rule can apply in these syntactic words. *Essui-glace*, for instance, is referentially opaque; *glace* does not denote a specific *glace* in a domain of interpretation. It has the generic interpretation characteristic of X^0s. Moreover, no referential element can replace *glace*. The expressions in (3) are ill formed in that they contain referential expressions, the quantified NP *quelques glaces* and the pronoun clitic *les*:

(3) a. *essui-quelques-glaces
        wipe-some-windshields
    b. *les-essui
        them-wipe

Hence syntactic words (phrases reanalyzed as words) differ from listed syntactic objects (idiomatic phrases) with respect to syntactic atomicity. That syntactic atomicity does not hold in full generality for listed syntactic objects follows from the fact that they are not X^0s. Syntactic words are X^0s and thus syntactic atoms.

In fact both syntactic words and listed syntatic phrases are idiomatic; that is, they are listed and have noncompositional meanings. Their difference is structural; the syntactic words are X^0s and exhibit syntactic atomicity, whereas the listed phrases are X^{max}s and exhibit syntactic transparency.

4.1.2 A Nonmorphological Word-Creating Rule

Syntactic words display the general properties of words (that is, distribution and atomicity), and for this reason we call them X^0s, but they do not have morphological form; unfortunately they manifest syntactic form.

Morphology is essentially useless in providing insight into their internal structure.

For example, neither components of the syntactic words in (1b–d) could possibly be the head of its respective word because neither one is a noun. The right-hand member of the words in (1a) might be analyzed as the head, assuming that the Right-hand Head Rule of Williams (1981) and chapter 2 also applies to French and that their structure is as follows:

(4)   N

     /\\
   V   N

(N → V N)

Clearly, though, this is accidental; the nouns in (1a) are not the semantic heads of the phrases that contain them (an *essui-glace* 'windshield wiper' is not a type of *glace* 'glass'). This analysis does not capture the generalization that the words in (1) all have a V + complement form; further, the correct result is obtained only for the cases in (1a). To account for (1b–d) we would need to add the following rules, for which the Right-hand Head Rule does not work:

(5) a. N → V A
   b. N → V Adv
   c. N → V P

We can draw a more accurate picture of these units if we assume that the structure of these objects includes a syntactic phrasal category. However, we want to preserve the predictions discussed earlier (distribution and atomicity) that followed from calling these X^0s. We may attain both objectives—syntactic form but world distribution—by positing the following rule:

(6) N → VP

Clearly V is to be considered the head of VP and not of N in (6). The question remains whether N has VP as its head. Certainly N cannot have VP as its head in the ordinary sense because "head of" is transitive, and the V of the VP is not the head of N. Further, the VP and the N disagree in features, and the object and its head ordinarily must agree in features. Still, there is a sense in which VP is the head of the N. We think it might be appropriate to consider VP the head, but a featurally atomic head; that is, its features are not percolated.

For example, plural number marked on the verb does not pluralize the dominating N, and in fact the result is ungrammatical: **essuient-glace*. These are to be distinguished from listed phrases such as *timbres-poste* 'postage stamps', cases that Selkirk (1982) analyzes as words (having a morphological structure); but we feel such forms have syntactic structure and in fact are not X^0s because they are head-initial.

This analysis can be supported in two ways. First, we can support the dominating lexical node in (6) by observing that the words in question can be inserted into X^0 positions and display syntactic opacity, as we have already seen.

The dominated syntactic phrasal node can be defended as well. In general the internal syntax of these items is characteristic of phrases. For example, the right-hand noun in the examples in (1a) can be analyzed as an internal argument of the V it is associated with, and θ-role assignment is done as in syntax. This is the case of *glace* in *essui-glace*, which has the θ-role Theme, given the properties of the verbal predicate *essui*, the head of the VP. Similarly, the left-hand member of the words in (1b–d) are verbal head predicates associated with a modifier bearing an adjunct θ-role. According to this analysis, the structure of these words is as follows:

(7)

In our view rule (6) is a marked rule with respect to the morphological laws. It creates words from phrases "by fiat," not by virtue of endowing them with morphological structure, which they manifestly do not have. Rule (6) is a nonmorphological word-creating rule of the periphery of the grammar.

Consider what we would lose if these examples were simply assimilated to other cases of word formation and described entirely without reference to the syntactic component. Suppose that the word formation component were enriched not with rule (6) but rather with all the rules necessary to generate (1a–d) directly, claiming that all the examples in (1a–d) manifest morphological form. Essentially the syntactic component would have to be imported into morphology. Further, it would remain unexplained why these words were deviant with respect to headedness.

But rule (6) fits well in the the model of grammar that distinguishes a core from a periphery and allows for the existence of marked rules. Under our analysis (6) is a marked rule of the grammar of French that accounts for the fact that some Ns are made of VPs. This is also a marked option in the grammar of languages such as English and Italian. The V Prt nominals of English, such as *push-up* and *breakdown*, and the V N nominals of

Italian, such as *copri-fuoco* 'curfew' and *rompi-testa* 'puzzle', are examples of marked syntactic words. We will assume that rule (6) is also part of the periphery of the grammar of English and Italian.

It now appears that French (and no doubt Spanish) lacks compounding altogether. Once we have subtracted fixed syntactic phrases (idioms) such as *timbres-poste* and phrases reanalyzed as words (syntactic words) such as *essui-glace*, there are no candidates left.

We believe that Selkirk (1982) misanalyzed fixed phrases such as *timbres-poste* as "left-headed compounds" (p. 21), thus concluding that French morphology is a mixture of left- and right-headed structures (since affixation in French is clearly right-headed). This is a clear example of a generalization compromised by the failure to properly separate syntax and morphology. With the listed syntactic phrases and the phrases reanalyzed as words removed, French morphology can be regarded as strictly right-headed.

4.1.3 Generalizing the Rule

Rule (6) describes the form of a subclass of syntactic words. We can extend it to cover cases like (8), which contain overt syntactic units such as NP and PP:

(8) a. trompe-l'oeil, fend-la-bise, coupe-la-soif
    b. boit-sans-soif, pince-sans-rire, monte-en-l'air
    c. bon-à-rien, haut-de-forme, juste-au-corps
    d. homme-de-paille, boule-de-neige, arc-en-ciel
    e. hors-la-loi, sans-le-sous, hors-d'oeuvre

The expressions in (8) are X^0s and therefore syntactic atoms, just as the cases in (1) were. This is shown by the ungrammaticality of (9) involving *trompe-l'oeil* (lit. 'deceive the eye') and by the fact that no reference assignment rule can apply to the NPs they contain:

(9) a. *trompe-souvent-l'oeil
              often
    b. *l'oeil trompe e
    c. *L'oeil a été acheté un trompe e par Jean
            was   bought   by Jean

These examples exhibit quite a broad range of simple phrasal forms. Again, if morphology were enriched to generate these directly, not only would the generality of morphological principles be compromised but the fact that all the examples in (9) are compatible with the laws of French syntactic form would be missed.

Because they contain overt XP complements, the words in (8) exhibit more sharply the "phrasal" nature of the interior of this kind of word. The NP complements in (8a) satisfy the subcategorization properties of the Vs they are associated with and can be analyzed as internal arguments of the verbal predicate. As for the PP complements in (8b), they either satisfy the subcategorization properties of the Vs they are associated with, or they qualify as modifiers of the verbal predicate in the same way as PPs in an ordinary VP. Similarly, examples (8c–e) can be analyzed as head and complement structures.

As in the case of (6), morphological principles are of little use in shedding light on these structures. For example, the left-hand member of these words is the head of the internal structure in some sense but not the head of the unit as a whole; the word as a whole is not headed by either member.

Some further rules of the kind given in (6) are needed for the cases in (8): N → AP, N → NP, and N → PP. They generalize to the following rule which accounts for all the cases:

(10) N → XP

The general rule (10) says that in French any syntactic unit can be analyzed as an N. This rule generates the following structures and expresses the properties that we have discussed:

(11)

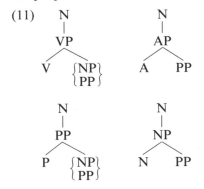

Of course the phrases actually found as X^0s are quite limited and short. In part this can be explained in terms of atomicity—because they are X^0s, they cannot contain any referential material, and it is difficult to construct a long phrase without including any referential material.

4.1.4 Governing Principles
In effect we have said that the form of the words we have been describing is given not directly in morphology but rather by syntactic rules. The only

"morphology" involved is the reanalysis of a phrase as a word. So the French expressions are not compounds in the sense in which English has compounds. Let us consider the exact cost of describing these directly by rules of morphology itself.

One might mistakenly propose, for example, that in French morphological objects are generally subject to the principles that bear on the well-formedness of syntactic structures. For instance, one could decide that there are no words like the following because French is a head-initial language:

(12) a. $*\begin{Bmatrix} \text{NP} \\ \text{PP} \end{Bmatrix}$ V   (*l'oeil-trompe, *sans-soif-boit)

    b. *PP A   (*à-rien-bon)

    c. *PP N   (*de-neige-boule)

    d. $*\begin{Bmatrix} \text{NP} \\ \text{PP} \end{Bmatrix}$ P   (*la-loi-hors, *d'oeuvre-hors)

Continuing in this vein, one might explain that words such as those in (13) are impossible by assuming that case theory, including the Case Filter, applied within word structure:

(13) a. *N NP   (*homme-la-paille)

    b. *A NP   (*bon-le-rien)

    c. Case Filter: *NP if NP is lexical and has no case.

One might then exclude the impossible cases in (14) by assuming that government must hold between a head and its complement within a word, as suggested by Di Sciullo (1981). The structure (14a) is excluded because the V does not govern the Comp position. (14b) is excluded because V does not govern sentence adverbs such as *nécessairement*, and (14c) is excluded because no government relation holds between the V and its external argument:

(14) a. *Comp V   (*qui-trompe, *à quoi pense)

    b. *Adv V   (*nécessairement-boit, *boit-nécessairement)

    c. *NP V   (*l'oeil-trompe, *la-bise-fend)

One must also suppose that the phrasal base rules apply in morphology, to explain, for example, why *le* precedes *oeil* in (8a).

Such suppositions create exactly the confusions that we are addressing in this chapter and in this text. Such an importation of all of syntax into morphology destroys the potential for any kind of generality in the laws of morphology, and no doubt of syntax as well.

Different grammatical principles bear on the well-formedness of syntactic and morphological objects. The definition of "head of phrase," for instance, expressed by the X-bar schema (15), cannot apply to words in general:

(15) $X^n \rightarrow \ldots X^{n-1} \ldots$

The head in words is determined left to right, not by decrements in bar level. Further, as mentioned earlier, French is strictly right-headed apart from the forms under discussion, and this strong generalization would have to be given up if the forms in (1) and (8) were morphological.

Moreover, case theory cannot apply with generality within words. If it could, structures such as $[N\ N]_N$ and $[A\ N]_N$, which are well formed in many languages, including English and Italian, would be excluded.

In fact there is no need to invoke case theory within morphology proper to account for the impossibility of the word structures in (11), nor to government within morphology proper to exclude the ill formed word structures in (14), if we suppose that these words contain syntactic phrases that are naturally subject to the principles of syntax. This "isolates" the importation of syntactic principles into morphology in rule (6) and avoids the general confusion that would result from the kind of importation we have just outlined.

Such confusion surfaces in several analyses of synthetic compounds (for example, Botha 1980, Fabb 1984) such as *meat-eating*, compounds that echo the internal structure of phrases in having a head-complement structure but differ from them in a number of properties. Botha discusses Afrikaans synthetic compounds such as *leeu-byter* 'one who bites lions' and suggests that they are derived by two types of rules. First, the base rules yield deep structures such as (16), and a lexical affixation rule attaches an affix to the derived deep structure, as in (17); the result is listed in the lexicon. Botha (1980, 67) expresses the interaction of the rules as follows: "The affixation rules are part of the lexicon and apply to the deep structure phrases that are fed into the lexicon by the base component":

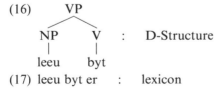

(16)   VP

     NP   V   :   D-Structure
     | |
     leeu   byt
(17) leeu byt er   :   lexicon

We would certainly prefer to exclude this kind of analysis because it implies that certain rules of morphology regularly interact with syntax. We feel that Botha's examples fall within the theory of compounding outlined in chapter 2 and that the attractiveness of his analysis of Afrikaans compounds—deriving from the fact that Afrikaans is syntactically verb-final—is misleading, because English, which is verb-initial (in VP), has exactly the same kind of compounds.

Fabb (1984, 134) argues that "synthetic compounds . . . are construed in the syntax" and that, more generally, most affixation is done in the syntax, and he provides some extensions of X-bar rules in syntax that permit the following structures:

(18)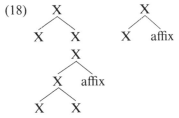

Fabb's proposal constitutes an extreme case of intermingling of syntax and morphology, with all the undesirable consequences that we have discussed, because the full generality of both morphological and syntactic rules must be abandoned in such a theory.

In our view most of the supposedly syntactically derived words, such as the synthetic compounds, are purely morphological; the few cases that remain, such as English *push-up* and French *essui-glace*, are best regarded as phrases reanalyzed as words by the marked rule Y → XP. This rule allows us to keep the morphological laws in their full generality without affecting the restrictiveness and the specificity of the morphology and the syntax. Moreover, it allows us to maintain the claim that syntactic rules and principles bearing on the well-formedness of syntactic structure apply within words only in the special case of phrases that have been reanalyzed as words.

There is an important difference between the compounds just discussed (*lion biter*) and the lexicalized (listed) phrases (phrasal idioms) discussed earlier. Compounds that receive a verbal interpretation involving θ-role assignment by the right member to the left member are a subset of the general class of compounds that includes, for example, *lapdog*, which do not involve θ-role assignment. So the link of θ-role assignment is simply a special case of the general class of links that compounds exhibit. Now we know that the relation of a verb to its object is always one of θ-role assignment—this relation does not exhibit the general range of links that we find in compounds. Thus it is no accident that formally phrasal words (like *essui-glace*) exhibit only the narrow link we call θ-role assignment and not the general class of links characteristic of compounds.

We think that the rule in (10) exactly sums up much information about these items—they have the distribution and atomicity of words but the form of phrases. And (8) also allows us to maintain the separation between the laws and rules governing words and phrases, laws and rules whose generality is threatened by efforts to treat syntactic words as instances of direct morphology. At stake is nothing less than the definitions of "head" in the respective theories and the mechanisms of case theory and θ-theory.

4.2   Coanalysis

Finally, we turn to cases of interpenetration that cannot be viewed as phrases reanalyzed as words and for which we will need a further mechanism; again, we will want a mechanism that does not give up what we have gained by the strict theoretical separation of syntax and morphology.

Coanalysis, a concept introduced by Williams (1979) for the analysis of the French causative construction, arises simply from possibilities already present in grammar. Syntax provides two ways of assigning various kinds of "marks" to phrases. Something can either be adjoined to the phrase as a whole or be marked on the head of the phrase. For example, in English the preposition *to* is adjoined to NPs (by the rule PP → P NP) to mark them as dative, whereas in Latin dative case is marked on the head:

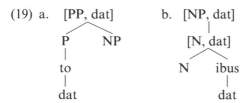

(19) a.   [PP, dat]   b.   [NP, dat]

The percolation is determined by the definition of "head" in both cases, and so far there is no cause for alarm—these examples simply show that language has two ways to do this kind of marking.

The difficulty arises because language sometimes wants to do both of these at once—this we will call *coanalysis*. How could a marker be both adjoined to a phrase as a whole and attached to its head? Clearly this is impossible in a single structure; however, if the head is peripheral in the phrase, that is, on one end or the other, then an affix could be ambiguously viewed as either affixed to the head or adjoined to the entire phrase:

(20)

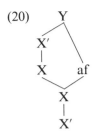

Here the affix is either syntactically adjoined to X' to give Y (the top analysis) or morphologically added to Z to give X (the bottom analysis). We think that certain constructions can be profitably viewed as involving such dual analyses, or coanalysis.

Coanalysis is a highly circumscribed phenomenon. First, both analyses of a coanalysis structure must be able to exist independently and meet whatever conditions analyses must meet in the language. Second, coanalysis involves no movement or scope assignment rules. Third, coanalysis is available only in very special circumstances—because the affix must be ambiguously taken as adjoined to the phrase and affixed to the head, coanalysis is available only if

(21) a. the affix is a suffix and X' is head-final, or
 b. the affix is a prefix and X' is head-initial,

for only under these circumstances could the structural ambiguity arise. We will call this the *Head Peripherality Condition*; note, however, that this is not an independent condition but arises because coanalysis is simply structural ambiguity.

4.2.1 The English Possessive
The English possessive illustrates certain properties of a coanalyzed structure rather well. First, the affix sometimes appears to attach to the possessor phrase as a whole, as observed by Bloomfield (1926):

(22) [the man on the corner]$_{NP}$'s hat

In other cases it seems to attach to the head N:

(23) their hat

In attaching to the entire phrase, the possessive is radically different from the plural marker, which never does this:

(24) *I saw [three men on the corner]s

That the marking in (22) is on the whole phrase and not just the last noun (*corner*) can be shown by the fact that when the last noun in similar cases is a pronoun, suppletion is not found:

(25) a. [the picture of him]$_N$'s frame

     b. *[the picture of his]$_{NP}$ frame

The suppletion only occurs on the head of the possessor phrase.

So the possessive marker sometimes attaches to the whole phrase (22) and sometimes strictly to the head (23). Actually we think that the best cases occur when it does both, that is, when the string can be coanalyzed:

(26)

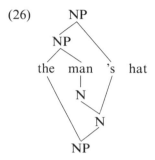

This coanalysis will be possible of course only when the possessor phrase is head-final. We feel that this is why (22) is so odd-sounding—it cannot be coanalyzed. The opposite of (22)—where the marker attaches only to a nonfinal head—is completely ungrammatical:

(27) a. *[the man's on the corner] hat

     b. *[his who likes corn] appetite

          (cf. [he who likes corn]'s appetite)

Why is this construction coanalyzed and not others? We might imagine that it is a feature of the possessive marker itself—it has two subcategorizations, one for NP (a syntactic one) and the other for N (a morphological one), and they can only be simultaneously met in a coanalyzed structure. The syntactic one is "stronger" in that it absolutely cannot be ignored, as (27) shows, whereas the morphological one can be, as (22) shows.

One can readily see how this coanalyzed structure came about historically—the first stage is the adjunction of a syntactic marker of possession to the phrase as a whole:

(28) [[John]$_{NP}$ his]$_{NP}$ hat

At this stage the structure is purely syntactic. The pronoun gets reduced to 's but is still affixed to the whole possessor NP; the reduced form, but the affix is still adjoined to the whole NP. This reconstrual is abetted by the fact that prenominal modifiers are in general head-final, thus permitting ambiguity of attachment. At this point coanalysis enters the picture, as a means of representing the dual status of the marker as an affix and as an item syntactically adjoined to the whole phrase. Coanalysis is not core grammar, it is simply the best you can do under certain circumstances.

4.2.2 The French Causative Construction

Williams (1979) proposes that the French causative construction is best viewed as a "coanalyzed" structure,[5] and the notion "coanalysis" was devised specifically to aid in the analysis of this construction. The notion "coanalysis" was meant to replace the rule of Thematic Rewriting of Rouveret and Vergnaud (1980).

For the French causative system, the word *faire* is the analogue of the English possessive: it is ambiguously both the first member of a compound verb and a main verb taking a complement. Consider the sentence *Jean a fait lire ce livre à Marie* 'Jean made Marie read this book':

(29)

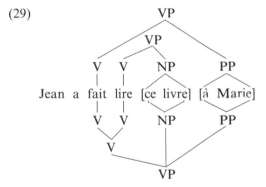

The top half of the analysis is purely syntactic, and the bottom one involves morphology. In this case the morphology is a rule of compounding.

Different languages exhibit each of the two causative structures that we assert hold simultaneously in French. English, for example, displays the purely syntactic one:

(30) John made me leave

Turkish and Japanese exhibit the purely affixal causative. In Japanese, the suffix *-sase* attaches to a verb to form a causative. The derived verb takes

---

5. Zubizarreta (1985) adopts the analysis of the French causative construction presented by Williams (1979) and repeated here, as well as the notion of coanalysis and the dual-tree representations of coanalyzed structures.

the external argument of the original verb as an internal (dative or accusatively marked) argument of the V + *sase* complex, by virtue of the "functor" status of *-sase* set out in chapter 2; the external Agent argument of *-sase* becomes the external argument of the V + *sase* complex:

(31) V (A̲, Th) +
      -sase (A̲) functor =
      V + sase (A̲' (A, Th))

As the first member of a compound verb, *faire* in French does just what *-sase* does in Japanese: it internalizes the original external argument:

(32) V (A̲, Th) +
      faire (A̲) functor =
      faire + V (A̲' (A, Th))

The internalized Agent is again realized as a dative, as specified again by a language-particular rule on the realization of internalized arguments. This is how we arrive at the bottom analysis of the coanalysis of this structure.

However, *faire* is simultaneously an independent verb that takes syntactic complements. This is the source of the top analysis of the construction. Because *faire* as an independent verb is not morphologically added, it does not alter the argument structure of the embedded verb in this analysis; rather it takes its complements as corresponding to its own θ-role(s), as any verb would, and assigns an Agent θ-role to its subject. The result is that the same θ-roles are assigned to the same items in both analyses, but the route is different. The object, for example, gets its θ-role "Theme" directly from the embedded verb in the top analysis, but it gets the role "Theme" from the complex verb *faire-lire* in the bottom analysis.

This feature of the analysis mimics the Thematic Rewriting rule of Rouveret and Vergnaud (1980). We consider our view a slight improvement on theirs because it has as a consequence that the "input" and "output" of Thematic Rewriting must be valid θ-structures, although they are different θ-structures. Their account could mimic this feature of ours by saying that the Projection Principle requires that the θ-Criterion be met both before and after Thematic Rewriting. We feel that this would not be correct because the causative construction violates the spirit of the Projection Principle in that θ-roles are assigned differently at different levels, and it violates the letter of the Isomorphy Principle of Sportiche (1984). We would insist that the Projection Principle hold within but not across analyses of a coanalysis—this is consonant with our view that the two parts of a coanalysis are not two stages of a single derivation but are actually two derivations.

The coanalysis view provides some explanations for peculiar features of the construction. For example, that the embedded verb precedes its subject follows from the Head Peripherality Condition on coanalyses discussed earlier, which follows from the fact that an item may ambiguously attach to a head or its phrase only if the head is peripheral in the phrase. The embedded verb must be adjacent to *faire* to be construed as morphologically compounded with *faire* in the morphological (bottom) analysis. This requirement forces the causatives of intransitives to exhibit the presumably marked order V VP NP. We illustrate with *Jean a fait rire Pierre* 'Jean made Pierre laugh':

(33)

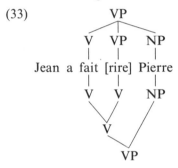

This somewhat marked order is apparently tolerated; otherwise the co-analyzed structure would be impossible. One might say again that this was the best French could do under the circumstances and not pretend that V VP NP is an optimal order of constituents in French.

Sometimes the syntactic analysis will simply be V VP, when the embedded verb does not take an external argument; this is the case in the *faire-par* construction, based on the passive infinitive of the verb, and in the causativization of raising verbs—neither passive nor raising verbs take external arguments:

(34) a. Jean a fait [devenir son fils bon professeur] 'Jean made his son become a good teacher'
   b. Jean a fait [frapper Pierre par Paul] 'Jean made Paul hit Pierre'

Also easily explained is that the causative construction permits reflexive clitics to be attached to the embedded verb, but not nonreflexive clitics, as Kayne (1975) observes and explains, though in different terms than we will here:

(35) a. *Jean a fait le   tuer à Pierre
        Jean made him kill   Pierre
     b. Jean a fait se   tuer à Pierre
        Jean made himself kill   Pierre
        'Jean made Pierre kill himself'

We think that the answer to this puzzle concerns the property that words are referentially opaque in the sense discussed in section 3.3—that is, words cannot contain items that refer. So the problem with (35a) is that the "word" (in the morphological analysis) *fait-le-tuer* contains a referential item and thus has the same status in French as the English compound *him-destroyer*. This property surely derives from the atomicity thesis— reference is defined for certain syntactic objects, such as NP, but is not defined in morphology at all. The reflexive clitic *se*, however, is not independently referential in the same way that *le* is; it is always bound to the external argument of the verb to which it is attached. We might then expect to find it inside of words, as in English compounds like *self-destroyer*. So the word *fait-se-tuer* does not contain an independently referential item and thus satisfies the prohibition against such items occurring inside words.

Earlier we contrasted the Japanese causative with the French, claiming that the Japanese was simply affixal, whereas the French was coanalyzed. The Japanese causative may also involve coanalysis. In that language, as opposed to French, the affixal analysis of the causative morpheme (-*sase*) is well motivated. So the question is, is the syntactic analysis of a coanalysis well motivated? A coanalysis of a typical Japanese causative would look like this (illustrating with *Tanaka ga John ni hon o yomi sase masu* 'Tanaka makes John read the book'):

(36)

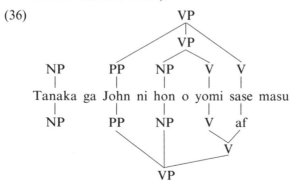

The evidence in favor of the syntactic half of the coanalysis is that the embedded Agent (*John ni*) acts like a subject in binding reflexives. The syntactic analysis provides just the right mechanism for this:

(37) Tanaka ga John ni [zibun o V]$_{VP}$ sase
                   self

The embedded VP in the syntactic analysis, the VP marked in (37), can itself bind the reflexive to its "subject" variable (as in Williams 1977), thus giving the correct interpretation.

The one troublesome feature of this analysis is that the reflexive will be correctly bound in only one of the two analyses—(the syntactic one, in (36); in the morphological analysis the reflexive is not contained in a VP that takes *John ni* as its subject:

(38) Tanaka ga [John ni zibun o Vsase]

Because (37) is grammatical, the reflexive *need not be properly bound in both analyses* of a coanalysis—one will do. This is especially worrisome because it was necessary earlier to apply the θ-Criterion to both analyses. Why both for the θ-Criterion but either one for the binding theory? This question must be answered.

4.2.3 Nominalizations

We feel that a certain kind of nominalization found in SOV (and presumably VSO) languages is a good candidate for coanalysis. In these languages certain (verbal) suffixes nominalize a sentence as far as its external distribution is concerned but not as far as its internal structure is concerned—that is, internally it still looks like an S. Under ordinary assumptions this should be impossible—for the nominal features on the verbal suffix to affect the nominality of the whole S, they would also have to infect every intervening node, because a feature on an affix can be registered in higher constituents only by the percolation mechanism that is entailed by the definition of "head" (see chapter 2).

For example, in Hopi (as reported in Jeanne 1978, 270) the suffix -*qa* nominalizes sentences:

(39) Niʔ mi-mi-y totimhoy-mi-y pima timalaʔyyin-qa-t namotiʔyta
     I   that   boys   they work-qa-oblique know
     'I know that the boys work'

But the interior syntax of these sentences is not nominal. Because of this, Jeanne hypothesizes an essentially coanalyzed structure for these—she says that -*qa* is a "defective noun" and lists a number of nominal properties that it has. But of course it is also a suffix on verbs. A coanalysis demonstrating both roles for -*qa* might be as follows:

(40)

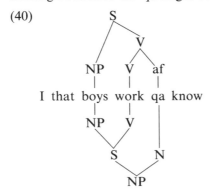

For this to work, -*qa* must have two rather different statuses: first, as a verbal affix that does *not* nominalize the verb to which it attaches and, second, as a regular noun.

What makes this coanalysis possible is that Hopi is an SOV head-final language—otherwise there could not be this systematic ambiguity between verbal suffix and head noun. In general this kind of nominalization can exist only in verb-final languages (or verb-initial languages with ambiguous prefixes). It cannot occur in English.

Lefebvre and Muysken's (forthcoming) account of Quechua nominalization points to another instance of coanalysis. Quechua is not strictly SOV, but, significantly, all of its nominalized clauses are. One nominalizer is the suffix -*sqa*, as in the following example (from Lefebvre and Muysken, forthcoming, chap. 2, (16)):

(41) [xwan papa- ta   mikhu sqa] n ta   yacha ni
     Juan potato ACC eat   NOM 3 ACC know I
     'I know that Juan eats potatoes'

Once can tell that the entire clause is nominalized because it takes case—the second *ta* is an accusative marker on the entire clause. One can also tell that the interior of the clause is not nominalized because the verb assigns nominative and accusative cases, which true nouns do not do; actually there is a "true" (unambiguous) nominalizer in Quechua (the suffix -*na*) that we know *does* nominalize the verb to which it attaches, because the verb so derived takes nonaccusative objects and genitive subjects (see Lefebvre and Muysken, sec. 2.2).

The assignment of the coanalyzed structure to (41) is straightforward, looking exactly like the coanalysis of the suffix -*qa* in Hopi:

(42)

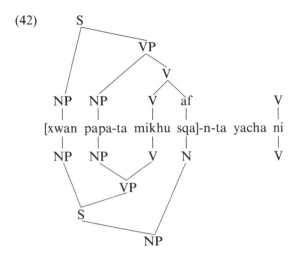

Similar things are apparently found in Japanese (with *-koto*) and Turkish.

The special character of such nominalizations derives from the ambiguity of the nominalizer (simultaneously verbal suffix and head noun), and the fact that such nominalizations are found only in verb-final languages (or at least only in verb-final structures) derives from the requirement that coanalyzed structures be head-peripheral.

4.2.4 The Italian Restructuring Constructions

The so-called restructuring constructions of Italian can be viewed as coanalyzed structures. These constructions typically involve *volere* 'want', modals such as *potere* 'can', *dovere* 'must', aspectuals such as *cominciare* 'start', *continuare* 'continue', *finire* 'finish', and motion verbs such as *venire* 'come', *andare* 'go', and *tornare* 'come back'. Rizzi (1982) points out that these verbs trigger a set of syntactic processes: clitic climbing (43), impersonal *si* passives (44), and the *avere/essere* 'to have/to be' alternation (45):

(43) a. Paulo vuole parlarti di politica
      b. Paulo ti vuole parlare di politica
          'Paulo wants to talk to you about politics'

(44) Ben presto, si comincierà a parlare di politica
      'Very soon, we will start talking about politics'

(45) a. Gianni ha dovuto tornare in Francia
      b. Gianni e dovuto tornare in Francia
          'Gianni had to go back to France'

Rizzi gives a unified account of these constructions in suggesting the existence of a restructuring rule, specific to Italian syntax, that is triggered by a restructuring verb. The rule transforms a bisentential structure into a simple clause, creating a verbal complex consisting of the verbs of both the main and embedded clauses:

(46) a. Paulo vuole [parlare di politica]
     b. Paulo [vuole parlare] di politica

Rizzi gives several arguments to justify the verbal complex structure created by restructuring. This complex may contain adverbs and complementizers but no other types of categories:

(47) a. Paulo vuole continuamente parlare di politica
        'Paulo wants always to talk about politics'
     b. Gianni comincierà presto a preparare la cena
        'Gianni will start soon to prepare supper'
     c. Maria deve assolutamente continuare a parlare di questo
        'Maria must absolutely continue to talk about this'
     d. Maurizio andrà spesso a trovare la sua amica a Torino
        'Maurizio will go frequently to visit his friend in Torino'
     e. *Paulo vuole di politica parlare
        'Paulo wants about politics to talk'
     f. *Gianni comincierà la cena a preparare
        'Gianni will start supper to prepare'
     g. *Maurizio andrà chi a trovare
        'Maurizio will go who to visit'

Coanalysis is a likely candidate for the analysis of these constructions, rather than a rule of restructuring, because the latter violates the Projection Principle: the restructured S-Structure form is not isomorphic to the original D-Structure form in terms of θ-role assignment and no doubt some other lexical properties.

The coanalysis view of the *volere* type of construction is well motivated in Italian, because it involves simultaneous syntactic and morphological analyses of the construction, both of which arise from possibilities already present in Italian grammar.

First, note that coanalysis is "optional" because the purely syntactic analysis is available by itself (the same could be said of the French *laisser* construction). *Volere* may select a tensed clause, as in (48a), and no coanalysis is involved; (48b) and (48c) are excluded by the Principle A of the binding theory:

(48) a.　Fabbrizio　vuole che　Paulo parla con Lucia
　　　　　'Fabbrizio want　that Paulo talks to　Lucia'
　　 b.　*Fabbrizio lo　　vuole che e parla con Lucia
　　　　　　　　　　him
　　 c.　*Fabbrizio gli　　vuole che Paulo parla e
　　　　　　　　　　to her

However, *volere* may select a VP complement, as in (49a), and coanalysis can apply because the structure (49b) is well formed (we will consider clitic climbing to be a diagnostic for coanalysis in the *volere* type of construction):

(49) a.　Gianni vuole parlare a Paulo
　　　　　'Gianni wants to talk to Paulo'
　　 b.　Gianni gli vuole parlare e
　　　　　'Gianni wants to talk to him'

As before, coanalysis obtains when an item has two subcategorization frames, a syntactic one and a morphological one (as in the case of the possessive *'s* of English and the French *faire*). We will assume further that *volere* triggers coanalysis because it syntactically selects a VP and morphologically selects a V. In coanalysis these c-selections are met simultaneously, as in (50):

(50)

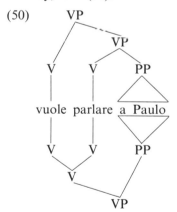

That *volere* takes a VP complement in the syntax has been argued by Manzini (1983), for instance, so the syntactic part of the analysis can be justified for Italian independent of coanalysis.

The morphological half of the analysis is justified as well, because Italian has morphological structures consisting of a VV complex, such as the nominal in (51):

(51) il   fare scrivere delle poesie
      'the make-write of   poetry'
      (N → V V) (or perhaps V → V V, a headed rule, and N → V)

This example contains an N composed of two Vs; it cannot be analyzed as
a gerund containing a VP because the direct object is not accusatively
marked but rather is introduced by a preposition. This provides evidence
for the morphological part of the analysis of the *volere* type of construction
presented above, independent of coanalysis.

However, the fact that adverbials can intervene between the two Vs in
the verbal complex, as in (47), could be viewed as a problem for the
coanalysis hypothesis, because the adjacency condition required by the
morphological half of such an analysis would be violated. But this problem
disappears if we assume that [Adv V] or [V Adv] structures can be morphological structures. The nominals in (52) provide empirical evidence for this
claim:

(52) a. Il [tutto fare] di Maurizio annoia Paulo
          the all-doing   of Maurizio annoys Paulo
     b. L'[alsarsi preso]   di Gianni disturba Maria
          the waking up early of Gianni disturbs Maria

Under this view *volere* type constructions with intervening adverbs, such
as (53a), have the structure in (53b):

(53) a. Maurizio vuole soltanto parlare con Mario
          Maurizio wants only   to talk to   Mario
          'Maurizio only wants to talk to Mario'

   b.

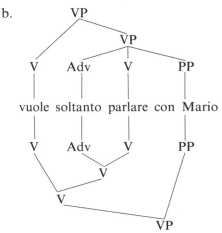

The possibility of an adverb within the *volere* verbal complex follows from the fact that Adv V can be construed as a word in the morphology. Further, it is expected that nonreferential elements such as adverbs may be contained within words because it follows from the referential opacity of words only that words may not contain referential elements.[6]

Our analysis also predicts that no PP can intervene between *volere* and the other verbal element in the verbal complex because PP contains a referential NP as object:

(54) *Gianni vuole a Roma parlare con Paulo
      Gianni wants in Rome to talk to Paulo

It has been noted by Di Sciullo (1981) that French and Italian differ from English in that adverbs can intervene between a V and its subcategorized complements:

(55) a. Il mange rapidement ses   pâtes
        he eats   quickly   his   pasta
     b. Il va   rarement   au   cinéma
        he goes   rarely   to the cinema
     c. Scrivera   subito   a   Maria
        he will write immediately   to Maria
     d. Divorava   spaventevolemente la pasta asciútta
        he devoured scaringly   the pasta

The well-formedness of these structures follows without further stipulations such as adverb-lowering rules and without giving up the requirement of adjacency of the V and object if we assume the morphological unit [V Adv]:

(56)

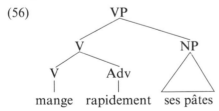

6. We cannot explain why the complementizers *a*, *di*, and *per* can intervene in the [V...V] complex where V is an aspectual or a motion V, except that it follows from referential opacity that nonreferring elements such as complementizers can occur within words:

(i) Paulo lo comincierà a leggere domani
    Paulo it will begin to read   tomorrow
    'Paulo will begin to read it tomorrow'

This analysis is motivated independently in French (and Italian) morphology by the presence of syntactic words with [V Adv] structure (see section 4.2.1).

Returning to the Vx verbs triggering coanalysis, the hypothesis that the [Vx Adv V] complex is a word in the morphological part of the analysis explains why there can be no linking of an element within the complex predicate with an element outside. The contrasts in the following examples illustrate this point. Discontinuous elements such as terms of degree—*così...che* 'as...as', *più...che* 'more...than', *meno...che* 'less...than'—cannot appear in the *volere* V structures or in the *volere* Adv V structures:

(57)

Paulo $\left\{\begin{array}{l}\text{*volera}\\ \text{preferiva}\\ \text{desiderava}\end{array}\right\}$ più parlare di   politica che di   linguistica

Paulo $\left\{\begin{array}{l}\text{wanted}\\ \text{preferred}\\ \text{desired}\end{array}\right\}$ more to talk about politics than about linguistics

(58)

Paulo $\left\{\begin{array}{l}\text{?volera}\\ \text{preferiva}\\ \text{desiderava}\end{array}\right\}$ più spesso parlare di   politica che di   linguistica[7]

Paulo $\left\{\begin{array}{l}\text{wanted}\\ \text{preferred}\\ \text{desired}\end{array}\right\}$ more often to talk about politics than about linguistics

In our system this contrast follows from syntactic atomicity, which prohibits sentence grammar rules from referring to the interior of words.

Further, the differences between Italian and French *volere/vouloir* constructions with respect to clitic climbing, shown in (59) and (60), follow as well:

(59) a.   Paulo lo   vuole vedere e
          Paulo him wants to see
          'Paulo wants to see him'
     b. *Paulo vuole lo vedere e

7. *Desiderare* 'desire' and *preferire* 'prefer' take a complementizerless infinitival complement, as does *volere*, but do not allow clitic climbing:

(i) a. Paulo desidera vedere Maria
          Paulo desires   to see Maria
     b. *Paulo la   desidera vedere
          Paulo her desires   to see
          'Paulo desires to see her'

(60) a. *Paul le   veut   voir   e
         Paul him wants to see
         'Paul wants to see him'
     b. Paul veut le voir e

In the Italian case *volere*... *V* has only one argument structure, because it is a complex predicate in the morphology, whereas French *vouloir* is a predicate with an independent argument structure, which does not form a verbal complex with the following infinitival V. If we assume that the binding domain for a category is the minimal θ-domain with respect to the predicate P that takes that category as an argument, where the minimal θ-domain is the minimal domain containing all arguments of P, then the only possible binding relation involving (cl, e) in the French case is (60b). In the Italian case the θ-Criterion is satisfied in the *volere*... *V* complex predicate in the morphological structure if we assume that the subject of *volere* controls the subject of V, in the sense of argument control discussed in chapter 2.

Under this view *volere*... *V* has only one external argument, and it has all the internal arguments of its associated V. The θ-Criterion is also satisfied in the syntactic part of the coanalyzed structure because when *volere* selects a VP, it s-selects an Event (E) θ-role, and it has the following argument structure:

(61) ($\underline{A}$, E)

The θ-Criterion is then satisfied by both the top and the bottom representations of the coanalyzed structures. In the top representation *volere* selects a VP complement, to which it assigns its Event θ-role; it also assigns the Agent θ-role to its external argument, saturating its argument structure. In the bottom analysis *volere* c-selects a V and forms a complex predicate with that V. *Volere* is a functor of the V it selects in the sense of section 2.2.2. Therefore the arguments of the V become internal arguments of the *volere* + V complex. The external argument of the embedded verb is controlled by the external argument of *volere*, so that argument is satisfied. The *volere* + V complex has only one external argument, the Agent θ-role of *volere*. An example is given in (62):

(62)

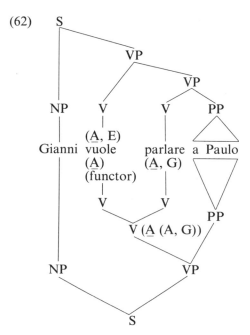

The Italian *volere* construction, then, in the morphological half of its analysis, is exactly like the analysis of the Japanese suffix *-tai* described in section 2.2.2.4.

4.2.5   Function Composition under Compounding

There is a fundamental difference between the cases of coanalysis in French and Italian on the one hand and the case in Japanese on the other. In French and Italian, the matrix verbs involved in the constructions (*faire/ fare*, *vouloir/volere*) are free forms (not affixes), whereas in Japanese the matrix "verb" is a suffix (*-sase*).

The status of *faire/fare*, *vouloir/volere* as free forms was established in (50)–(52), where it was shown that adverbs may intervene between *fare* and the embedded verb; adverb intervention between the embedded verb and *-sase* in Japanese is impossible:

(63) *iki kinoo -sase
       go today make
       'make go today'

The same point can be made with coordination; coordination of embedded predicates can take place under *faire*, but not under *-sase*:

(64) a. J'ai fait partir Jean et   arriver Pierre
         I made leave Jean and arrive Pierre
         'I made Jean leave and Pierre arrive'
     b. *Sake o nomu to   sakana o tabe -saseta
         sake   drink and fish   eat make
         'I made someone drink sake and eat fish'

These facts are clearly connected with the affixal status of *-sase* and the nonaffixal status of *faire*; they immediately raise the question whether the morphological analysis of the Romance constructions is still available. At first glance the Romance causative construction seems entirely outside the range of any kind of morphological analysis because it involves coordination. But in fact compounding admits coordination, as the following freely generated examples attest:

(65) book and magazine rack
     up and down chopper
     picnic and dance coordinator
     fish and vegetable plate

So if *faire* + V is conceived of as a case of compounding (the union of two free forms), there is no obstacle to coordination under *faire: faire* + *V and V*.

A problem remains, however. In the linear string that is to be coanalyzed, as in (64a), *V and V* does not appear as a connected substring (*Jean* intervenes); so even if coordination is allowed under compounding, it is not clear why the compounding analysis would be applicable. But this probably results from a general feature of coordination; the compounding *is* possible if the example is represented in an across-the-board format of the kind proposed by Williams (1978b):

(66) J'ai fait $\begin{Bmatrix} \text{partir Jean} \\ \text{arriver Pierre} \end{Bmatrix}$ et

In the across-the-board format *fait* is adjacent to both *partir* and *arriver* as well as *et*, so the compounding may take place.

In Japanese, of course, coordination is blocked because *-sase* is a bound form, and coordination is prohibited under bound forms.

This last explanation is threatened by the existence of some cases of coordination under bound forms:

(67) pro and anti abortion (forces)
     super and supra national
     pro Reagan and Bush

Perhaps these prefixes have achieved a tentative status as a kind of free form, for in most cases this is impossible:

(68) *indecisive and discreet (meaning 'indiscreet')
      *educate and rehabilitation
      *compact and completeness

So it seems that we can readily instantiate the intuition that *faire* is a free form and *-sase* is not, in our theory. The independent theory of coordination permits coordination among free forms but not among bound forms.

An immediate conclusion about the general theory presented in chapter 2 emerges: because *faire* is not an affix, function composition is not limited to affixes but is also found in compounds, even though there are no such cases in English. In fact it would be surprising if function composition were not found in compounds, because it is found in affixal forms and in syntax. Why should it skip over compounds?

4.3 The Phonological Word

Thus far we have systematically ignored a fourth type of word, the phonological word, which we will discuss briefly here mainly for contrast with the notions of word that we have called *morphological object* and *syntactic atom*. A simple example is the English modal contractions:

(69) a. John should've/could've come
      b. I'll come

Let us suppose that *I'll* is a word in some phonological sense; of course *'ll* by itself is not a possible phonological word. The question then becomes, Is it a word in any other sense?

The answer is no. It is not a morphological word because no rules of morphology will effect this combination: *I* is not an argument of *'ll*; there is no θ-relation between the two parts. Nor is *I'll* a syntactic atom. The fact that it contains a referential pronoun shows this. Also, there is no syntactic category to which *I'll* could be assigned that would correctly account for its distribution. It is not a verb or auxiliary because it does not have the distribution of verbs or auxiliaries (**Bob I'll come*), and it is not an NP because it does not have the distribution of an NP. Similar conclusions hold for *should've*.

It differs strikingly, then, from even the cases of coanalysis considered in the previous section. In all those cases there were grounds for the morphological half of the analysis—the θ-relation between *faire* and the complement verb was characterizable in terms of morphological rule, as described in chapter 2.

The correct distribution for *I'll* is obviously arrived at in this way: first, independently determine the distribution of *I* and *will* according to syntax, and then weld the two together when they occur juxtaposed. Clearly, if this description is correct, then *I'll* is not a syntactic atom in any sense, because it is composed of syntactically accessible parts. So if *I'll* is a word at all, it is a word in yet a fourth sense of "word": it is a phonological word.

There is further evidence that *I'll* is not a syntactic unit. It does not submit to syntactic rules:

(70) *Who'll does Bob think t win

Similarly for *should've*, as noted by Selkirk (1972):

(71) *Should've Bob won

Should've contrasts with *don't*, as Selkirk (1972) has observed:

(72) Don't they win

The contrast is principled: *don't* is a syntactic object and, unlike *should've*, has a syntactic distribution. It has the same distribution as *do*—in fact it can cooccur with *not*:

(73) Don't not go

Should've does not have a syntactic distribution; that is, the rules of syntax (minus the "welding" rule) are powerless to describe its distribution.

The Romance clitics present a particularly thorny case. Is the unit cl + V a syntactic atom (and morphological object) or simply a phonological word? Both sides have been taken. Grimshaw (1982) in particular has taken the position that the cl + V unit is lexically derived, and has a syntactic distribution.

There is good evidence leading to Grimshaw's conclusion. The clitic is often the object of the verb, meaning that a θ-relation holds between them, which means that a lexical rule like the one we have invoked for noun incorporation can derive the cl + V unit as a morphological object:

(74) le + mange $(\underline{A}, \text{Th}) \rightarrow \text{le}_i \text{ mange } (\underline{A}, \text{Th}_i)$

(See Grimshaw 1982 for an elaboration of this proposal.)

Most analyses of the Romance clitics, beginning with that of Kayne (1969), have taken the clitic to be syntactically accessible and therefore not a component of a morphological object. This position is consistent with the late phonological welding of the clitic to the verb, yielding cl + V as a phonological word.

With both accounts available, how do we choose? How does the child choose?

That the clitic attaches to the auxiliary verb appears at first to favor the syntactic analysis, because the clitic bears no θ-relation to the auxiliary verb and hence could not be joined with it by morphology:

(75) Jean l'a mangé
       Jean it ate
       'Jean ate it'

However, this simple conclusion is obstructed by good evidence for rules in Romance that reanalyze the auxiliary and main verbs together as a complex verb; if this complex verb inherits the θ-structure of the main verb, then it is quite possible to say that the clitic *is* θ-related to the complex verb, thereby permitting a morphological derivation in which the clitic is joined to the complex verb (*a-mangé*) by satisfying one of its arguments:

(76) le$_i$ a   mangé
              \ (A, Th)
               _⌣_/
       V (A, Th$_i$)

However, there is evidence from Italian that this is not correct. In Italian the clitic may appear before or after the verb, depending on whether the verb is infinite or finite:

(77) a. Gli   voglio scrivere
           to him I want to write
           'I want to write to him'
      b. Voglio scrivere gli

This alone is reason enough to question the affixal analysis of these clitics, because they are not determinately prefixal or suffixal. But the analysis becomes impossible when we consider infinitive auxiliaries:

(78) Voglio averlo   visto
       I want to have it seen
       'I want to have seen it'

Here the clitic is attached to the auxiliary, and because it intervenes between the auxiliary and main verbs, it cannot be understood as attached to a complex verb formed of the auxiliary and main verbs. This is a clear case of an affix attached to an item of which it is not an argument, so we must conclude that clitics are syntactically attached to the things with which they form a phonological unit.

So Romance clitics, unlike the cases of noun incorporation considered in chapter 3, are not morphological—they govern syntactic positions. It is then no surprise that they differ in another way from cases of noun incorporation. When a clitic is moved, a double of the clitic may sometimes be left behind, but the double must be in a different (case) position from the one the clitic is moved from ("Kayne's generalization"):

(79) Lo vimos *(a) Juan (Spanish)
     him we see   Juan
     'We see Juan'

Here the clitic is accusative, so the accusative case position in syntax must be vacant, and the direct object obligatorily appears with the a case marker. In the case of noun incorporation, as we saw in section 3.6.3, no restriction was imposed on the manner of expression of the syntactic direct object by the fact that incorporation had taken place.

So, as linguists equipped with the theory of morphological object in chapter 2, we can determine that Romance clitics are not joined to verbs by morphological rule. But how does a child conclude this, rather than concluding that Romance clitics are simply a sort of degenerate case of noun incorporation? Perhaps the child can identify the strict complementarity of clitic objects and full objects. Giving the child the ability to observe complementarity is not in keeping with the general dictum of "no negative evidence" and would seem to require that the child save examples. But before observing the complementarity, the child will have observed that the direct object has two syntactic realizations, clitic and full, and perhaps under this special circumstance a brief search for complementarity could ensue without jeopardizing the child's general program of drawing conclusions only from positive examples.

4.4 Conclusion

In this chapter we have introduced successively more and more intermingling of syntax and morphology, and the reader may have the uneasy feeling that we have quickly undone everything that we have argued for in the first three chapters. This is not so, and a quick review of the situation will reveal why.

In effect we have introduced two new analyses—the analysis of syntactic words, which involves rules of the form $X \rightarrow YP$, and the analysis of coanalyzed structures, which involves no new rules but does involve dual simultaneous analyses.

In neither case have we allowed intermingling of the rules in the two systems. In the case of syntactic words we have "encapsulated" the intrusion of syntax into morphology in the one rule X → YP, which by itself does not entail any further intermingling than the rule itself expresses. In the case of coanalysis we have maintained that each analysis of a coanalyzed structure must be well formed by the existent rules of the grammar, independent of what happens in the other analysis, and further, that each analysis by itself must respect the atomicity thesis—only when the two analyses are viewed together may one speak of intermingling. In neither situation does any syntactic rule analyze a morphological object or syntactic atom. Thus the arrangement defended in chapter 3 is maintained.

We feel that this is the most conservative treatment available for the phenomena discussed in this chapter, giving up the least amount of the predictive power of the atomicity thesis and the general articulation of the theory into two subtheories, syntax and morphology.

It is quite easy to think of approaches to these problems that give up everything. For example, suppose that in the face of syntactic words, we simply imported syntax into morphology, creating one grand science of the word/phrase, with no separation. (We of course would then have no need of syntax itself, because morphology would generate everything syntactic that we might need.) Or suppose that in the face of the facts concerning coanalyzed structures, we introduced into syntax parts or all of morphology. If we are wrong in our conclusions, then perhaps this is the correct theory. In any case it is clearly quite a different theory from the one outlined here, even including syntactic words and coanalysis.

Such a theory, consisting essentially of the union of the rules and laws of syntax and morphology, will treat the hierarchy of units discussed in chapter 1 (from morpheme through word to sentence) as unbroken, all of a theoretical piece. The opacity of words will in essence be an island condition, specifying that the items below a certain point on the hierarchy are opaque with respect to the operations defining the higher units. The different definitions of "head" (bar-decrement versus right/left) will be sorted out among the various elements. The failure of units above the level of word to appear in the formation of units below the level of word must be explained in some way, although the existence of syntactic words could be cited as evidence that this is a false generalization. And so on.

However, if we are correct in our conclusion that syntax and morphology are parallel but independent subcomponents, then we must ask why this is so, why there is not one grand science of the word/phrase. But on this question we do not have a speculation.

Bibliography

Allen, M. (1978). "Morphological Investigations." Doctoral dissertation, University of Connecticut, Storrs.

Anderson, S. (1982). "Where's Morphology?" *Linguistic Inquiry* 13, 571–612.

Aronoff, M. (1976). *Word Formation in Generative Grammar*. MIT Press, Cambridge, Mass.

Aronoff, M. (1983). "Potential Words, Actual Words, Productivity, and Frequency." In S. Hattori and K. Inoue, eds., *Proceedings of the 13th International Congress of Linguists*. Tokyo.

Bach, E. (1979). "Control in Montague Grammar." *Linguistic Inquiry* 10, 515–531.

Baker, M. (1983). "Noun Incorporation in Iroquoian." Ms., MIT, Cambridge, Mass.

Baker, M. (1985). "Incorporation: A Theory of Grammatical Function Changing." Doctoral dissertation, MIT, Cambridge, Mass.

Baker, M. (1985a). "The Mirror Principle and Morphosyntactic Explanation." *Linguistic Inquiry* 16, 373–415.

Bloomfield, L. (1926). "A Set of Postulates for the Science of Language." *Language* 2, 153–164. [Reprinted in M. Joos, ed. (1957). *A Reader in Linguistics I*. University of Chicago Press, Chicago, Ill.]

Borer, H. (1984). "The Projection Principle and Rules of Morphology." In *Proceedings of the Fourteenth Annual Meeting of NELS*. GLSA, University of Massachusetts, Amherst.

Botha, R. P. (1980). "Word Based Morphology and Syntactic Compounding." In *Stellenbosch Papers in Linguistics* 5.

Bradley, D. (1980). "Lexical Representation of Derivational Relations." In M. Aronoff and M.-L. Kean, ends., *Juncture*. Anma Libri, Saratoga, Calif.

Chomsky, N. (1955). *The Logical Structure of Linguistic Theory*. Ms. [Published 1975 by Plenum, New York.]

Chomsky, N. (1970). "Remarks on Nominalization." In R. Jacobs and P. Rosenbaum, eds., *Readings in English Transformational Grammar*. Ginn, Waltham, Mass.

Chomsky, N. (1973). "Conditions on Transformations." In S. Anderson and P. Kiparsky, eds., *A Festschrift for Morris Halle*. Holt, Rinehart and Winston, New York.

Chomsky, N. (1981). *Lectures on Government and Binding*. Foris, Dordrecht.

Chomsky, N., and H. Lasnik (1977). "Filters and Control." *Linguistic Inquiry* 8, 425–504.

Di Sciullo, A. M. (1980). "N and X′ Theory." In *Proceedings of the Tenth Annual Meeting of NELS*. Department of Linguistics, University of Ottawa, Ontario. [*Cahiers linguistiques d'Ottawa* 9.]

Di Sciullo, A. M. (1981). "Sur les composés verbaux du français." *Revue de l'association québecoise de linguistique* 1, 45–59.

Di Sciullo, A. M. (1981a). "On Strict Subcategorization." *Proceedings from the Tenth Symposium on Romance-Languages*. Georgetown University Press, Washington, D.C.

Di Sciullo, A. M. (1983). "Théorie du liage et expressions idiomatiques." *Revue de l'association québecoise de linguistique* 3.2.

Di Sciullo, A. M. (1985). "A Note on Clitics." Ms., Université du Québec à Montréal.

Di Sciullo, A. M. (1986). "Sur la définition des variables." *Revue de l'association québecoise de linguistique* 5.2.

Emonds, J. (1969). "Root and Structure Preserving Transformations." Doctoral dissertation, MIT, Cambridge, Mass.

Fabb, N. (1984). "Syntactic Affixation." Doctoral dissertation, MIT, Cambridge, Mass.

Farmer, A. (1980). "On the Interaction of Morphology and Syntax." Doctoral dissertation, MIT, Cambridge, Mass.

Fiengo, R. (1974). "Semantic Conditions on Surface Structure." Doctoral dissertation, MIT, Cambridge, Mass.

Grimshaw, J. (1982). "On the Lexical Representation of Romance Reflexive Clitics." In J. Bresnan, ed., *The Mental Representation of Grammatical Relations*. MIT Press, Cambridge, Mass.

Gruber, J. (1965). "Studies in Lexical Relations." Doctoral dissertation, MIT, Cambridge, Mass.

Halle, M. (1973). "Prolegomena to a Theory of Word Formation." *Linguistic Inquiry* 4, 3–16.

Hewitt, G. (1903). "Iroquoian Cosmology." In *Twenty-first Annual Report of the Bureau of American Ethology*.

Hornstein, N., and A. Weinberg (1981). "Case Theory and Preposition Stranding." *Linguistic Inquiry* 12, 55–91.

Jackendoff, R. (1975). "Morphological and Semantic Regularities in the Lexicon." *Language* 51, 639–671.

Jaeggli, O. (1980). "Spanish Diminutives." In F. H. Nuessel, ed., *Contemporary Studies in Romance Languages*. Indiana University Linguistics Club, Bloomington, Ind.

Jaeggli, O. A. (1986). "Passive." *Linguistic Inquiry* 17, 587–622.

Jeanne, L. (1978). "Aspects of Hopi Grammar." Doctoral dissertation, MIT, Cambridge, Mass.

Kayne, R. (1969). "The Transformational Cycle in French Syntax." Doctoral dissertation, MIT, Cambridge, Mass.

Kayne, R. (1975). *French Syntax*. MIT Press, Cambridge, Mass.

Kisseberth, C. W., and M. I. Abasheikh (1977). "The Object Relationship in Chi-Mwi:ni, a Bantu Language." In P. Cole and J. Sadock, eds., *Syntax and Semantics 8: Grammatical Relations*. Academic Press, New York.

Lapointe, S. (1979). "A Theory of Grammatical Agreement." Doctoral dissertation, University of Massachusetts, Amherst.

Lefebvre, C., and P. Muysken (forthcoming). *Nominalizations in Quechua*. Reidel, Dordrecht.

Lieber, R. (1980). "On the Organization of the Lexicon." Doctoral dissertation, MIT, Cambridge, Mass.

Lieber, R. (1983). "Argument Linking and Compounds in English." *Linguistic Inqiury* 14, 251–285.

Manzini, M. R. (1983). "Restructuring and Reanalysis." Doctoral dissertation, MIT, Cambridge, Mass.

Marantz, A. (1985). "On the Nature of Grammatical Relations." Doctoral dissertation, MIT, Cambridge, Mass.

Milsark, G. (1974). "Existential Sentences in English." Doctoral dissertation, MIT, Cambridge, Mass.

Mithun, M. (1983). "The Evolution of Noun Incorporation." *Language* 60, 847–894.

Montalbetti, M. (1984). "After Binding: On the Interpretation of Pronouns." Doctoral dissertation, MIT, Cambridge, Mass.

Moortgat, M. (1984). "A Fregean Restriction on Metarules." In *Proceedings of the Fourteenth Annual Meeting of NELS*. GLSA, University of Massachusetts, Amherst.

Muysken, P. (1981). "Quechua Causatives and Logical Form: A Case Study in Markedness." In A. Belletti, L. Brandi, and L. Rizzi, eds., *Theory of Markedness in Generative Grammar*. Scuola Normale Superiore, Pisa.

Pesetsky, D. (1979). "Russian Morphology and Lexical Theory." Ms., MIT, Cambridge, Mass.

Pesetsky, D. (1985). "Morphology and Logical Form." *Linguistic Inquiry* 16, 193–248.

Postal, P. (1962). "Some Syntactic Rules of Mohawk." Doctoral dissertation, Yale University, New Haven, Conn.

Reinhart, T. (1983). *Anaphora and Semantic Interpretation*. Croom Helm, London.

Rizzi, L. (1982). *Issues in Italian Syntax*. Foris, Dordrecht.

Roeper, T. (1987). "Implicit Arguments and the Head-Complement Relation." *Linguistic Inquiry* 18.2.

Roeper, T., and M. E. A. Siegel (1978). "A Lexical Transformation for Verbal Compounds." *Linguistic Inquiry* 9, 197–260.

Rouveret, A., and J.-R. Vergnaud (1980). "Specifying Reference to the Subject." *Linguistic Inquiry* 11, 97–202.

Selkirk, E. (1972). "The Phrase Phonology of English and French." Doctoral dissertation, MIT, Cambridge, Mass.

Selkirk, E. (1981). "Chapter 2." Ms., University of Massachusetts, Amherst.

Selkirk, E. (1982). *The Syntax of Words*. MIT Press, Cambridge, Mass.

Siegel, D. C. (1974). "Topics in English Morphology." Doctoral dissertation, MIT, Cambridge, Mass.

Sportiche, D. (1983). "Structural Invariance and Symmetry." Doctoral dissertation, MIT, Cambridge, Mass.

Stanners, R. F., J. J. Neiser, W. P. Herron, and R. Hall (1979). "Memory Representation for Morphologically Related Words." *Journal of Verbal Learning and Verbal Behavior* 18, 399–412.

Wasow, T. (1972). "Anaphoric Relations in English." Doctoral dissertation, MIT, Cambridge, Mass.

Williams, E. (1977). "Discourse and Logical Form." *Linguistic Inquiry* 8, 101–139.

Williams, E. (1978). "Passive." Ms., University of Massachusetts, Amherst.

Williams, E. (1978a). "Notes on Lexical Theory." Ms., University of Massachusetts, Amherst.

Williams, E. (1978b). "Across-the-Board Rule Application." *Linguistic Inquiry* 9, 31–43.

Williams, E. (1979). "The French Causative Construction." Ms., University of Massachusetts, Amherst.

Williams, E. (1980). "Predication." *Linguistic Inquiry* 11, 208–238.

Williams, E. (1981). "Argument Structure and Morphology." *The Linguistic Review* 1, 81–114.

Williams, E. (1981a). "On the Notions 'Lexically Related' and 'Head of a Word'." *Linguistic Inquiry* 12, 245–274.

Williams, E. (1984). "*There*-Insertion." *Linguistic Inquiry* 15, 131–153.

Williams, E. (1984a). "Grammatical Relations." *Linguistic Inquiry* 15, 639–673.

Williams, E. (1985). "NP Trace in Theta Theory." Ms., University of Massachusetts, Amherst.

Williams, E. (1985a). "PRO in NP." *Natural Language and Linguistic Theory* 3, 277–295.

Woodbury, T. (1977). "Greenlandic Eskimo, Ergativity, and Relational Grammar." In P. Cole and J. Sadock, eds., *Syntax and Semantics 8: Grammatical Relations*. Academic Press, New York.

Zubizarreta, M. L. (1985). "The Relation between Morphophonology and Morphosyntax: The Case of Romance Causatives." *Linguistic Inquiry* 16, 247–290.

Index

On the Definition of Word
*by Anna Maria Di Sciullo
and Edwin Williams*

The MIT Press
Massachusetts Institute of Technology
Cambridge, Massachusetts 02142

On the Definition of Word develops a consistent and coherent approach to central questions about morphology and its relation to syntax. In sorting out the various senses in which the word *word* is used, it asserts that three concepts that have often been identified with each other are in fact distinct and not coextensive: listemes (linguistic objects permanently stored by the speaker), morphological objects (objects whose shape can be characterized in morphological terms of affixation and compounding), and syntactic atoms (objects that are unanalyzable units with respect to syntax).

The first chapter defends the idea that listemes are distinct from the other two notions and that all one can and should say about them is that they exist. A theory of morphological objects is developed in chapter 2. Chapter 3 defends the claim that the morphological objects are a proper subset of the syntactic atoms, presenting the authors' reconstruction of the important and much-debated Lexical Integrity Hypothesis. A final chapter shows that there are syntactic atoms that are not morphological objects.

Anna Maria Di Sciullo is in the Département de Linguistique à l'Université du Québec à Montréal. Edwin Williams is in the Department of Linguistics at the University of Massachusetts. *On the Definition of Word* is Linguistic Inquiry Monograph 14.

DISOP
0-262-54047-9